Marketing: Theory, Practice and Perspectives

Dr. Qaisar Abbas Fatimi

Dedication

This book is dedicated to the pillars of my life—my friends, my family, and my students.

- Dr. Qaisar Abbas Fatimi

ABOUT THE AUTHOR

Dr. Qaisar Abbas Fatimi is a distinguished figure in the realm of marketing, whose extensive academic background and practical experience have established him as a leading expert in the field. Holding a Ph.D. in Marketing and an MBA in Digital Marketing, Dr. Abbas combines theoretical knowledge with real-world applications, offering unique insights into the evolving landscape of marketing.

With over a decade of experience, Dr. Fatimi has navigated the complexities of digital marketing, SEO, SEM, social media marketing, and analytics across various industries. His passion for bridging the gap between academic theory and practical execution has led to the development of innovative marketing strategies that have propelled businesses to new heights of success and visibility.

"Marketing: Theory, Practice, and Perspectives" reflects Dr. Fatimi's holistic approach to marketing. Through this work, he aims to demystify marketing concepts and practices, making them accessible to students, practitioners, and enthusiasts alike. His writing is infused with the belief that understanding the foundational theories of marketing is crucial to innovatively addressing the dynamic challenges of the digital age.

Beyond his professional achievements, Dr. Fatimi is deeply committed to mentoring the next generation of marketers. He is an advocate for continuous learning and encourages his readers and students to explore marketing not just as a business function but as a critical tool for connecting with and understanding the world around them.

Dr. Fatimi's contributions to the field of marketing extend beyond his work, as he actively participates in conferences, workshops, and as a volunteer, sharing his knowledge and fostering a community of like-minded individuals passionate about the power of marketing.

ACKNOWLEDGEMENT

Writing "Marketing: Theory, Practice, and Perspectives" has been a journey of exploration, learning, and passion—a journey that would have been considerably more challenging without the support and inspiration of many incredible individuals.

I would like to extend my heartfelt gratitude to my family, whose love, understanding, and sacrifices have been the backbone of my strength and perseverance. Your endless support has made all the difference, turning challenges into opportunities and dreams into reality.

To my esteemed colleagues and mentors in the field of marketing, thank you for your invaluable insights, constructive feedback, and scholarly contributions, which have enriched this book immensely. Your dedication to advancing our field is truly inspiring.

To my students, past and present, thank you for your curiosity, engagement, and the fresh perspectives you bring into the classroom every day. You are the reason educators like myself strive to be better, to learn more, and to teach with enthusiasm and purpose.

Lastly, I must acknowledge the countless authors, researchers, and practitioners whose works have informed and shaped the discourse of marketing. Your research and writings have been foundational to the creation of this book, providing a rich tapestry of knowledge from which I have drawn extensively.

This book is a tribute to all of you who have been part of my journey, in ways big and small. Your contributions, support, and faith have been indispensable to the realization of this work.

Dr. Qaisar Abbas Fatimi

ONLINE RESOURCES:

WWW.DIGITALMARKETINGWITHQAF.COM/MARKETING-THEORY-PRACTIVE-AND-PERSPECTIVES

CONTENTS

PREFACE

Imagine a small coffee shop in a quaint neighborhood, which, through the power of effective marketing, transforms into a global phenomenon. Picture a startup with a revolutionary idea, using just the right blend of marketing strategies to become a household name. These stories, and countless others, form the tapestry of marketing's rich and varied history, a tapestry this book aims to explore and elucidate.

At the heart of our journey is the quest to understand the essence of marketing. We begin in the past, delving into the foundational theories crafted by pioneers of the trade. These theories, like the story of David Ogilvy who revolutionized advertising with his focus on direct, customer-centric messaging, lay the groundwork for all that marketing has become today.

As we move through the chapters, we encounter the practices that have shaped the present landscape of marketing. We tell tales of companies like Nike, which harnessed the power of brand storytelling to build an empire, and of small businesses that leveraged social media marketing to compete with industry giants. These stories illuminate the practical applications of marketing theories, demonstrating their power and versatility.

In addressing ethical and sustainable marketing, we recount narratives of brands like Patagonia, which has woven environmental responsibility into its marketing fabric, inspiring a generation of conscious consumers and marketers alike. These tales underscore the growing importance of ethics in marketing, highlighting the shift towards more responsible business practices.

The digital revolution in marketing brings its own set of stories. We delve into the world of AI and VR, recounting how these technologies are creating new frontiers in customer engagement, much like how Spotify uses data analytics to personalize user experiences, redefining the music industry's marketing strategies.

Data-driven marketing strategies are no less dramatic. We explore how Netflix's data analytics have not just shaped marketing campaigns but also content creation, turning viewer preferences into blockbuster hits.

Our global perspective includes tales of cross-cultural marketing successes and faux pas, learning from brands that have skillfully navigated the complex tapestry of global markets, and from those who stumbled, offering invaluable lessons in the importance of cultural sensitivity.

As we peer into the future, we share predictions and possibilities, like the potential impact of blockchain technology on marketing transparency and customer trust. These forward-looking perspectives prepare our readers for the exciting, uncharted territories of marketing yet to come.

In crafting "Marketing: Theory, Practice, and Perspectives," the goal was not just to create a book but to weave a story – a story that captures the imagination, imparts wisdom, and inspires action. It is a story that invites you, the reader, to be a part of this incredible world of marketing, to learn from its past, engage with its present, and shape its future.

BRIEF OVERVIEW OF BOOK SECTIONS

Part I: The Essentials of Marketing
This section lays the foundation for understanding marketing. It begins by exploring the definition and evolution of marketing, emphasizing its critical role in modern business and how global events shape marketing strategies. Foundational theories are examined, presenting a journey from classic to modern marketing theories and models, and debating consumer-centric versus product-centric approaches. The rise of relationship marketing is highlighted, along with practical case studies. The section then delves into market research, presenting diverse methodologies, best practices, and innovative tools, followed by a comprehensive look at consumer behavior, covering aspects like psychology, social factors, decision-making, and the influence of technology. It concludes with a focus on ethics and social responsibility, advocating for ethical practices and integrating social responsibility into marketing strategies, underscoring marketing's role in addressing global challenges.

Part II: Strategies and Management in Marketing
This part of the book shifts focus to the strategic and managerial aspects of marketing. It starts with the essentials of crafting comprehensive marketing plans and strategic marketing processes, including agile strategies and cross-functional team integration. The STP framework (Segmentation, Targeting, Positioning) is explored in-depth, with an emphasis on advanced segmentation techniques like micro-segmentation and AI-driven positioning strategies. Product and brand management are then discussed, including navigating product life cycles and building brand equity. The section also covers pricing strategies and approaches, including dynamic and personalized pricing, and concludes with an examination of distribution

channels and the dynamics of logistics and supply chain management in marketing, especially in the context of e-commerce.

Part III: Advanced Marketing Practices and Digital Integration
This part addresses advanced marketing practices with a significant emphasis on digital integration. It begins with integrated marketing communication techniques, exploring the dynamics of various promotional tools and the role of social media and influencers. Digital marketing is then examined in the context of the modern era, highlighting online advertising, effective email marketing, content strategies, and the role of AI and machine learning in digital campaigns. The section also covers mobile marketing strategies and the impact of new technologies like AI and VR. Global marketing strategies are discussed, with a focus on international market entry, cross-cultural marketing, and contemporary global challenges.

Part IV: Measuring and Enhancing Marketing Performance
This part emphasizes the importance of data-driven marketing. It starts with the role of data in marketing, including leveraging marketing analytics for insights and evaluating marketing ROI. Ethical considerations and privacy issues in data-driven marketing are also addressed. The section then explores customer relationship management (CRM), discussing strategies for building lasting customer relationships and utilizing CRM systems and technologies. It concludes by addressing contemporary marketing challenges, such as navigating digital transformation and adapting to evolving consumer preferences and global marketing challenges.

Part V: The Evolving Landscape of Marketing
The final part of the book looks toward the future of marketing. It begins by identifying emerging trends and future directions, including sustainable and ethical marketing approaches and the potential impact of evolving technologies like blockchain. The book then provides concluding insights, synthesizing key takeaways from the evolution of marketing and envisioning future marketing practices. It emphasizes the importance of acquiring future skills and competencies in the marketing field.

MARKETING: THEORY, PRACTICE, AND PERSPECTIVES

Dr. Qaisar Abbas Fatimi

PART I: THE ESSENTIALS OF MARKETING

Coca-Cola's Polar Bear Campaign

(AI Generated Photo)

Coca-Cola's use of polar bears in its advertising campaign is a classic example of emotional marketing. Introduced in 1993, the polar bears were featured in a television advertisement called "Northern Lights." The bears, watching the aurora borealis and drinking Coca-Cola, captured the hearts of viewers with their human-like behavior and family bonds. These characters quickly became synonymous with the Coca-Cola brand, appearing in numerous ads and becoming a central part of Coca-Cola's holiday branding.

The polar bear campaign showcases Coca-Cola's expertise in creating emotionally resonant marketing. By consistently using these characters, Coca-Cola has not only humanized its brand but also formed a strong emotional connection with its audience. The campaign's success demonstrates the power of consistent branding and the impact of emotionally driven marketing strategies.

CHAPTER 1. INTRODUCTION TO MARKETING

Marketing is an ever-evolving discipline, essential to the success of any business. It's a dynamic force that combines creativity, strategy, and understanding of consumer behavior to create value for both companies and their customers. This chapter serves as a gateway into the world of marketing, laying the foundational knowledge necessary to navigate the subsequent discussions on marketing theories, practices, and perspectives. Through exploring the definition and evolution of marketing, understanding its role in modern business, and examining the impact of global events on marketing strategies, readers will gain a comprehensive overview of what marketing entails and why it is crucial in today's business landscape.

Marketing is not just about selling products or services; it's about creating stories that resonate with consumers, building relationships, and making a meaningful impact on society. As we delve into the history of marketing, we'll uncover how it has transformed from a focus on production and sales to a customer-centric approach that prioritizes meeting the needs and desires of consumers. This journey through time will highlight the key theories and figures that have shaped marketing into what it is today.

In examining marketing's role in modern business, we'll showcase how it intertwines with every aspect of a company, from product development to customer service. Successful companies like Apple have mastered the art of marketing, demonstrating how a well-crafted strategy can lead to unparalleled brand loyalty and market dominance.

Furthermore, the chapter will explore how global events, including the digital revolution and the COVID-19 pandemic, have led to significant shifts in marketing practices. These events have accelerated the adoption of digital marketing, emphasized the importance of agility and adaptability in marketing strategies, and highlighted the growing consumer demand for sustainability and social responsibility.

By the end of this chapter, readers will have a solid understanding of marketing's multifaceted role in shaping business success and societal change. This foundational knowledge will set the stage for deeper exploration into the strategic, ethical, and digital aspects of marketing that are reshaping the business world today.

1.1 EXPLORING THE DEFINITION AND EVOLUTION OF MARKETING

American Marketing Association (AMA) Definition:

"Marketing is the activity, set of institutions, and processes for creating, communicating, delivering, and exchanging offerings that have value for customers, clients, partners, and society at large."

Philip Kotler's Definition:

"Marketing is the science and art of exploring, creating, and delivering value to satisfy the needs of a target market at a profit. Marketing identifies unfulfilled needs and desires. It defines, measures, and quantifies the size of the identified market and the profit potential."

The Chartered Institute of Marketing (CIM) Definition:

"Marketing is the management process responsible for identifying, anticipating, and satisfying customer requirements profitably."

Marketing is a dynamic and multifaceted discipline that encompasses the strategies and tactics companies use to identify, engage, and satisfy customer needs, ultimately driving profitable transactions. Its definition has evolved over the years, adapting to changes in consumer behavior, technological advancements, and market conditions. At its core, marketing involves creating value for both the company and its customers through a variety of activities including product development, pricing strategies, distribution channels, and promotional efforts.

The Evolution of Marketing: From Production to Digital Age

The Production Era: In the early 20th century, marketing was primarily focused on production and distribution efficiency. Companies operated under the assumption that a good product would sell itself, with little emphasis on consumer needs or desires.

The Sales Era: As production capabilities improved and markets became saturated with products, businesses shifted focus towards selling and persuasion to unload their surplus inventory. This era saw the rise of advertising and salesmanship as key tools for attracting customers.

The Marketing Concept Era: Introduced in the mid-20th century, this era marked a significant shift towards a customer-centric approach. Businesses began to recognize the importance of understanding and meeting consumer needs as a pathway to success. This period emphasized market research, product differentiation, and targeted marketing campaigns.

The Societal Marketing Era: Emerging in the 1970s, this era expanded the marketing concept to include societal interests, advocating for the balance between company profits, consumer satisfaction, and public welfare. It highlighted the importance of ethical considerations and social responsibility in marketing practices.

The Relationship Marketing Era: Starting in the 1990s, the focus shifted towards building long-term relationships with customers rather than single transactions. This era emphasized customer retention, satisfaction, and loyalty as key drivers of business success.

The Digital Marketing Era: The advent of the internet and digital technologies has transformed marketing in the 21st century. This era is characterized by the rise of digital channels, social media, mobile marketing, and data analytics, offering unprecedented opportunities for personalized and interactive customer engagement.

The Role of Technology and Globalization

Technology and globalization have played significant roles in the evolution of marketing. The internet, social media, and mobile devices have opened new channels for communication and interaction, allowing brands to reach global audiences with unprecedented speed and precision. Data analytics and artificial intelligence have enabled deeper insights into consumer behavior, allowing for more targeted and effective marketing strategies.

1.2 MARKETING'S ROLE IN MODERN BUSINESS

In the dynamic landscape of modern business, marketing transcends its traditional boundaries, emerging as a pivotal force that drives innovation, shapes consumer perceptions, and fosters sustainable growth. This expanded role is a testament to the discipline's evolution, adapting to the rapid technological advancements, shifting consumer expectations, and the increasing demand for transparency and social responsibility. As we delve deeper into marketing's multifaceted influence on modern business, we uncover its critical function in not only promoting products or services but also in crafting compelling narratives, building robust relationships, and steering the business towards ethical and sustainable practices.

Navigating the Digital Transformation

The advent of digital technology has revolutionized marketing, introducing new channels and tools for engagement, personalization, and measurement. Digital marketing now stands at the forefront of a company's strategy to connect with its audience, leveraging data analytics to tailor messages and offers to individual consumer preferences. The success stories of brands like Netflix and Spotify, which use data to personalize content and enhance user experience, highlight the power of digital marketing in today's business landscape. Incorporating a discussion on the strategic use of SEO, content marketing, and social media platforms can provide readers with insights into effective digital marketing tactics that drive visibility, engagement, and loyalty.

Embracing Ethical and Sustainable Marketing

As consumers increasingly prioritize ethical considerations and sustainability, modern marketing must reflect these values in its practices and communications. Ethical marketing involves being transparent about product sourcing, manufacturing processes, and the brand's societal impact, building trust with consumers who seek authenticity and integrity. Sustainable marketing practices, exemplified by brands like Patagonia, go beyond the product to emphasize a company's commitment to environmental stewardship and social responsibility. Highlighting these aspects can illustrate how marketing not only influences consumer choice but also contributes to broader societal and environmental well-being.

Cultivating Global Connections

The global marketplace presents unique challenges and opportunities for marketing. Understanding cultural nuances, adapting strategies to local markets, and navigating regulatory environments are crucial for international success. Case studies of companies like McDonald's, which customizes its menu for different countries, can shed light on effective global marketing strategies that respect cultural differences while maintaining brand consistency. This section underscores marketing's role in bridging geographical and cultural divides, fostering a global brand presence that resonates with diverse audiences.

Measuring Success and Driving Innovation

In the modern business environment, marketing's effectiveness is closely tied to its ability to demonstrate return on investment (ROI) and drive innovation. The incorporation of marketing metrics and analytics allows businesses to measure success in concrete terms, refining strategies for greater impact. Furthermore, marketing's role in product development highlights its importance in identifying market needs and driving innovation. Apple's continuous innovation, supported by its marketing prowess, exemplifies how marketing and product development intersect to meet consumer demands and shape market trends.

Looking Towards the Future

As we contemplate the future of marketing, it is clear that emerging technologies like artificial intelligence (AI), augmented reality (AR), and virtual reality (VR) will further transform the discipline. These technologies offer new avenues for creating immersive and personalized brand experiences, suggesting an exciting horizon for marketing innovation. Additionally, the ongoing dialogue about privacy and data ethics in digital marketing points to the need for evolving marketing practices that prioritize consumer rights and data protection.

1.3 GLOBAL EVENTS AND MARKETING SHIFTS

The landscape of modern marketing is continually reshaped by global events, which challenge businesses to adapt swiftly and innovatively to maintain relevance and engagement with their audiences. From the digital revolution to the COVID-19 pandemic and the growing emphasis on sustainability, these pivotal moments have not only accelerated changes in consumer behavior but also underscored the resilience and agility of marketing strategies in the face of uncertainty. This section delves into how global events have catalyzed shifts in marketing practices, highlighting the adaptability and forward-thinking required to navigate these changes.

The Digital Revolution: A Paradigm Shift

The advent of the internet and subsequent digital technologies has ushered in a revolutionary shift in marketing. This era has transformed how brands connect with consumers, introducing digital channels that facilitate more direct, personalized, and interactive forms of engagement. The rise of social media platforms and digital advertising has democratized brand communication, enabling even small businesses to reach global audiences with unprecedented precision. An exploration of how companies like Amazon have leveraged e-commerce and digital marketing to dominate the retail space can offer insights into the transformative impact of the digital revolution on marketing strategies.

The COVID-19 Pandemic: Accelerating Digital Adoption

The COVID-19 pandemic has been a catalyst for rapid change, pushing businesses to accelerate their digital transformation efforts. With physical stores shuttered and consumers confined to their homes, the importance of online presence and e-commerce capabilities has never been more pronounced. Brands have had to pivot quickly, adopting digital tools and platforms to engage with their audiences, often in innovative ways. For example, fitness companies like Peloton experienced unprecedented growth by offering virtual classes, tapping into consumers' desire for connectivity and wellness in a time of isolation. This period has highlighted the need for agility in marketing strategies, with a focus on digital channels to reach and engage consumers effectively.

Sustainability and Social Responsibility: Responding to Consumer Demand

In recent years, there has been a significant shift towards sustainability and social responsibility in marketing, driven by growing consumer awareness and concern for environmental and social issues. Brands are increasingly expected to not only talk about sustainability but to demonstrate real commitment through their actions and business practices. Marketing strategies now often include messaging around eco-friendly initiatives, ethical sourcing, and contributions to social causes. Highlighting companies like Patagonia, which has built its brand around environmental activism and ethical practices, can illustrate how integrating sustainability into marketing strategies can resonate with consumers and differentiate brands in a crowded marketplace.

Navigating Cultural Sensitivities in a Global Marketplace

The globalization of markets presents both opportunities and challenges for marketing, particularly in navigating cultural sensitivities and tailoring messages to diverse audiences. Successful global marketing strategies require an understanding of cultural nuances, local consumer behaviors, and regulatory environments. The adaptation of global brands like Coca-Cola and McDonald's to local tastes and preferences underscores the importance of cultural sensitivity in marketing, ensuring that campaigns are relevant, respectful, and effective across different regions.

Preparing for Future Shifts: The Role of Innovation and Ethics

As we look to the future, marketing is set to evolve further, with emerging technologies like artificial intelligence, blockchain, and augmented reality offering new possibilities for consumer engagement. However, alongside these innovations, ethical considerations around data privacy, transparency, and inclusivity will become increasingly critical. Marketers must stay ahead of technological trends while ensuring their strategies uphold ethical standards and contribute positively to society.

CHAPTER 2. FOUNDATIONAL THEORIES IN MARKETING

This chapter delves into the bedrock of marketing as a discipline, exploring the foundational theories that have shaped the field over the years. These theories provide the essential framework for understanding how marketing strategies are developed, implemented, and refined to meet the evolving needs of consumers and the market. From the early emphasis on production and product quality to the modern focus on consumer needs, societal well-being, and relationship building, the evolution of marketing theories reflects broader changes in society, technology, and business practices.

We begin our exploration with a journey through classic marketing theories, examining how early concepts like the Production, Product, and Selling Concepts laid the groundwork for understanding market dynamics and consumer behavior. These theories highlight the evolution of marketing thought from focusing solely on production and product features to recognizing the importance of selling and persuasion in a crowded marketplace.

As we transition to modern perspectives, we encounter evolving marketing theories and models that respond to changes in consumer attitudes, technological advancements, and global challenges. The Societal Marketing Concept and Digital Marketing Theory represent significant shifts towards more ethical, sustainable, and technologically integrated approaches to marketing. These contemporary theories emphasize the importance of balancing profit with societal good and leveraging digital platforms for more personalized and engaging marketing communications.

The chapter also engages in the vital debate between consumer-centric and product-centric approaches. This discussion illuminates the ongoing dialogue within the field about the best path to business success, whether by focusing on the superiority of the product itself or by prioritizing the needs and desires of the consumer.

Further, we delve into the Rise of Relationship Marketing, a theory that has gained prominence in the digital age as businesses seek to build long-term relationships with their customers. This approach underscores the shift from transactional marketing, which focuses on single sales, to a more holistic strategy that values customer loyalty, satisfaction, and engagement over the long term.

Through a series of case studies, "From Theory to Action," we see these theories come to life. Companies like IKEA, Patagonia, and Zappos demonstrate how foundational marketing theories are applied in real-world scenarios, driving business success and innovation. These case studies not only illustrate the practical application of marketing theories but also highlight the diverse strategies companies employ to navigate the complexities of the marketplace.

By the end of this chapter, readers will have a comprehensive understanding of the foundational theories that underpin the field of marketing. This knowledge is crucial for both students and professionals as they seek to develop effective marketing strategies that are responsive to an ever-changing business environment. As we build on these theories throughout the book, readers will be equipped to appreciate the depth and breadth of marketing as a critical business function and a fascinating area of study.

2.1 A JOURNEY THROUGH CLASSIC MARKETING THEORIES

Embarking on a journey through the realm of classic marketing theories offers us an invaluable perspective on the evolution of marketing thought and its pivotal role in shaping contemporary practices. This exploration not only illuminates the foundational concepts that have guided the field but also connects the historical shifts to the intricate marketing landscape we navigate today.

The Product Concept: The Genesis of Marketing Thought

Originating in the late 19th and early 20th centuries, the Product Concept revolves around the belief that consumers will favor products offering superior quality, performance, or innovative features. This theory underscores the importance of product excellence and the intrinsic value of commodities. It reflects an era when the primary challenge for businesses was to enhance product quality and innovation to meet the basic needs and preferences of consumers. Pioneers like Henry Ford, with his revolutionary assembly line production of the Model T, epitomize this concept, demonstrating how product innovation can meet widespread consumer needs and shape industry standards.

The Production Concept: Efficiency and Availability

Closely related to the product concept, the Production Concept focuses on high production efficiency and widespread distribution. This approach gained prominence during the Industrial Revolution, a period marked by rapid advancements in manufacturing technologies and an expanding consumer market. The mantra of the production concept was simple: make products affordable and available to a broad audience. This theory is best illustrated by companies like Procter & Gamble and their efforts to make essential goods accessible to the mass market, showcasing how efficiency in production and distribution can create competitive advantage and consumer loyalty.

The Selling Concept: The Art of Persuasion

As markets became increasingly saturated, the Selling Concept emerged, emphasizing aggressive selling and promotional efforts to generate sales. This theory, prevalent from the 1920s to the 1950s, assumes that consumers require persuasion to purchase products. It highlights a period when businesses began to focus more on advertising and sales techniques to differentiate their products in crowded markets. This era's exemplar, Coca-Cola, utilized creative advertising campaigns to embed its products in the cultural zeitgeist, demonstrating the power of persuasion and brand building in driving consumer demand.

The Marketing Concept: A Paradigm Shift to Customer-Centricity

The Marketing Concept introduced a significant paradigm shift in the mid-20th century, moving towards a customer-centric approach. This theory advocates understanding and satisfying consumer needs better than competitors as the pathway to business success. It marked a departure from product and sales-focused strategies, emphasizing market research, target market segmentation, and integrated marketing strategies. The transition to this concept is vividly illustrated by the transformation of companies like IBM from product-oriented to customer-focused businesses, highlighting the shift towards strategic, research-based marketing practices centered on customer satisfaction.

The Societal Marketing Concept: Balancing Profit and Public Interest

Emerging in the 1970s, the Societal Marketing Concept expands on the marketing concept by incorporating the broader impact of marketing decisions on society's welfare. It advocates for the balance between company profits, consumer desires, and public interest, introducing ethical considerations and social responsibility into marketing practices. This era's approach is embodied by Ben & Jerry's, a company that has intertwined social activism with its business model, demonstrating how aligning marketing strategies with societal well-being can foster brand loyalty and societal impact.

2.2 MODERN PERSPECTIVES: EVOLVING MARKETING THEORIES AND MODELS

As the marketing landscape has evolved, so have the theories and models that underpin the discipline. The advent of digital technology, changes in consumer behavior, and a growing emphasis on sustainability and ethics have spurred the development of modern marketing perspectives. These contemporary theories and models build on classical foundations but adapt to the complexities of the global, digital marketplace.

Digital Marketing Theory

Digital marketing theory centers on the use of digital channels to promote products and services. This includes strategies across search engines, social media, email, websites, and mobile apps. The theory emphasizes the importance of data analytics and targeted content to engage consumers in more personalized and interactive ways. Key concepts include SEO (Search Engine Optimization), SEM (Search Engine Marketing), content marketing, and social media engagement, reflecting the shift towards inbound marketing tactics that attract customers through relevant and helpful content.

Consumer Relationship Management (CRM)

CRM theory focuses on managing a company's interactions with current and potential customers. It uses data analysis about customers' history with a company to improve business relationships, specifically focusing on customer retention and ultimately driving sales growth. Modern CRM integrates technology to automate processes, gather customer data, and implement marketing strategies that personalize the customer experience, fostering loyalty and long-term engagement.

Service-Dominant Logic

Service-Dominant Logic (SDL) represents a shift in marketing thought from a goods-centered view of market exchanges to one that sees service as the fundamental basis of exchange. This perspective emphasizes the co-creation of value between businesses and customers, where products are seen as platforms for service delivery. SDL suggests that the key to competitive advantage lies in the firm's ability to co-create unique value with its customers rather than from the intrinsic value of its output.

Integrated Marketing Communications (IMC)

IMC is a strategic approach that integrates various promotional tools and communications channels to provide a clear, consistent, and compelling message about the organization and its products. It underscores the importance of a unified message across all marketing channels, ensuring that all forms of communications and messages are carefully linked together. This holistic approach enhances the impact of marketing campaigns, ensuring that consumers receive consistent messages in every interaction with the brand.

Sustainability Marketing

Sustainability marketing goes beyond traditional marketing concepts by integrating social and environmental responsibility into the marketing process. It involves creating and promoting products and services that not only meet consumer needs but also contribute to the wellbeing of society and the environment. This perspective emphasizes the triple bottom line of people, planet, and profit, encouraging businesses to operate in a way that is economically viable, socially responsible, and environmentally friendly.

The Experience Economy

This theory posits that businesses must orchestrate memorable events for their customers, and that memory itself becomes the product — the "experience." More than ever, consumers are seeking and valuing experiences over tangible goods. Marketers, in response, are creating immersive brand experiences that engage customers in a profound and personal way. This can range from experiential marketing events to designing retail spaces that offer unique sensory experiences.

A brief of some of the key theories

Theory	Theorists	Main Tenets	Critics	Application
4 Ps of Marketing (Marketing Mix)	E. Jerome McCarthy	Marketing decisions are categorized into product, price, place, and promotion.	May be too simplistic, not accounting for service or customer experience.	Comprehensive marketing strategy development.
Consumer Decision Process	John Dewey	Consumers go through a process of problem recognition, information search, evaluation, purchase, and post-purchase evaluation.	Overlooks impulsive buying, more suited to high-involvement products.	Customer journey mapping, targeted marketing campaigns.
Relationship Marketing	Leonard Berry	Focus on long-term customer relationships rather than short-term sales and transactions.	Can be resource-intensive, difficult to measure ROI.	Customer retention strategies, loyalty programs.
Societal Marketing Concept	Philip Kotler	Marketing should deliver value to customers in a way that	Difficult to balance profitability with societal benefits.	Ethical and sustainable marketing practices.

Theory	Theorists	Main Tenets	Critics	Application
		maintains or improves both the consumer's and society's well-being.		
Service-Dominant Logic	Stephen Vargo & Robert Lusch	Services, rather than goods, are the fundamental basis of exchange; value is co-created with the customer.	May not apply as effectively to traditional product-based industries.	Service design, customer experience enhancement.
Brand Equity Theory	David Aaker	The value of a brand is based on the extent to which it has high brand loyalty, name awareness, perceived quality, strong brand associations, and other assets like patents.	Focusing too much on brand equity can neglect other business aspects.	Brand development, management, and valuation.
Diffusion of Innovations	Everett Rogers	Describes how, why, and at	Assumes homogeneity	Product launch strategies,

Theory	Theorists	Main Tenets	Critics	Application
		what rate new ideas and technology spread through cultures, with different types of adopters.	in consumer populations.	targeting early adopters.
AIDA Model	E. St. Elmo Lewis	Consumers move through stages of Attention, Interest, Desire, and Action when engaging with marketing.	Simplifies the complexity of consumer decision-making.	Advertising and sales strategies, content creation.
Blue Ocean Strategy	W. Chan Kim & Renée Mauborgne	Encourages creating new market space ('Blue Oceans') rather than competing in existing markets ('Red Oceans').	Risky, as creating new markets is challenging and unpredictable.	Market innovation, new product development.
Holistic Marketing	Philip Kotler	Integration of all marketing efforts (internal, integrated,	May be complex to implement, especially in	Comprehensive marketing strategy, corporate social

Theory	Theorists	Main Tenets	Critics	Application
		relationship, and socially responsible marketing) to ensure coherence.	smaller organizations	responsibility efforts

2.3 DEBATING CONSUMER-CENTRIC AND PRODUCT-CENTRIC APPROACHES

The debate between consumer-centric and product-centric approaches in marketing represents a fundamental strategic choice companies must navigate. Each approach offers distinct perspectives on how to achieve business success, influencing product development, marketing strategies, and overall business operations. Understanding the nuances, benefits, and limitations of each can help organizations tailor their strategies to meet market demands and consumer expectations effectively.

Product-Centric Approach

The product-centric approach, one of the earliest philosophies in marketing and business strategy, posits that the primary focus should be on developing superior products with unique features or quality. Companies adopting this perspective invest heavily in research and development, innovation, and product improvement, operating under the belief that a superior product will naturally attract customers.

Benefits:

Encourages innovation and excellence in product development.

Can lead to breakthrough products that define or redefine categories.

Focuses on product quality and features, which can attract a loyal customer base.

Limitations:

Risks ignoring shifting consumer needs and preferences, potentially making even superior products irrelevant.

May lead to an inward-looking culture that overlooks market trends and competitive dynamics.

Can result in marketing myopia, where companies are too focused on their products to adapt to market changes.

Consumer-Centric Approach

In contrast, the consumer-centric approach places the consumer at the heart of all business decisions, from product development to marketing and customer service. This strategy is rooted in the belief that understanding and meeting consumer needs and preferences is key to attracting and retaining customers. Companies adopting a consumer-centric approach invest in market research, customer feedback mechanisms, and personalized marketing to ensure their offerings resonate with target audiences.

Benefits:

Aligns product offerings with current consumer needs and preferences, increasing market relevance.

Facilitates stronger relationships with customers through personalized engagement and responsiveness.

Encourages flexibility and adaptability in business strategies, allowing companies to pivot based on consumer feedback and market trends.

Limitations:

Can lead to a dilution of product focus if trying to meet too many diverse consumer needs.

Requires significant investment in market research and consumer analysis to continuously gauge consumer preferences.

Risk of over-reliance on current consumer feedback, potentially missing out on breakthrough innovations that consumers cannot yet envision.

Balancing the Approaches

The debate is not about choosing one approach over the other but finding the right balance that leverages the strengths of both. Innovative companies like Apple have demonstrated the ability to blend product-centric innovation with a deep understanding of consumer needs, creating groundbreaking products that define entire categories while maintaining a strong consumer focus.

Integrating Feedback: Incorporating consumer feedback into the product development process can ensure that innovations meet market needs.

Market Sensing: Continuously sensing and responding to market trends can help product-centric companies stay relevant.

Product Leadership: Consumer-centric companies can strive for product leadership by focusing on a few key areas where they can truly excel and differentiate.

2.4 THE RISE OF RELATIONSHIP MARKETING

The rise of relationship marketing marks a significant shift in the focus of marketing strategies from transactional exchanges to the cultivation of long-term relationships with customers. This approach recognizes the value of customer loyalty and the benefits of sustained engagement over time, moving beyond the immediate sale to build a deeper, more meaningful connection with consumers. Relationship marketing emphasizes customer retention, satisfaction, and loyalty as key drivers of business success, leveraging personalized communication and customer service to foster a strong bond between the brand and its customers.

Foundations of Relationship Marketing

The concept of relationship marketing emerged in the late 20th century, as businesses began to understand the limitations of traditional, transaction based marketing models in a rapidly evolving market landscape. The foundational premise of relationship marketing is that retaining existing customers is more cost-effective and profitable than constantly acquiring new ones. This approach relies on understanding individual customer needs, preferences, and behaviors to tailor marketing efforts and create value for both the customer and the company over the long term.

Key Elements of Relationship Marketing

Customer Focus: At the heart of relationship marketing is a deep focus on the customer, with efforts aimed at understanding and meeting their specific needs and expectations.

Personalization: Personalized marketing messages and offers, based on customer data and insights, play a crucial role in making consumers feel valued and understood.

Communication: Ongoing, two-way communication with customers helps to build trust and loyalty. This includes not just promotional messages but also opportunities for feedback and engagement.

Customer Service: Exceptional customer service is pivotal in relationship marketing, with an emphasis on exceeding customer expectations and resolving issues promptly and effectively.

Loyalty Programs: Many businesses implement loyalty programs to reward repeat customers, encouraging continued patronage by offering discounts, exclusive offers, or other perks.

Benefits of Relationship Marketing

Increased Customer Retention: Satisfied customers are more likely to remain loyal to the brand, resulting in repeat business and reduced customer churn.

Higher Customer Lifetime Value: Long-term customers tend to spend more over time, contributing significantly to revenue and profitability.

Positive Word-of-Mouth: Loyal customers often become brand advocates, sharing their positive experiences with others and attracting new customers through word-of-mouth.

Competitive Advantage: Strong customer relationships can differentiate a brand in crowded markets, providing a sustainable competitive edge.

Challenges in Implementing Relationship Marketing

While the benefits are clear, implementing relationship marketing can present challenges. It requires a cultural shift within the organization towards customer-centricity, significant investment in customer relationship management (CRM) systems, and the ability to collect, analyze, and act on customer data effectively. Additionally, maintaining the personalization and high level of service expected in a relationship marketing strategy can be resource-intensive.

2.5 FROM THEORY TO ACTION: CASE STUDIES IN MARKETING

To illustrate the application of these theories in practice, we explore several case studies:

IKEA's Application of the Product Concept

IKEA's marketing strategy serves as a textbook example of the product concept in action. This concept suggests that consumers will favor products that offer the most quality, performance, or innovative features. IKEA has built its brand around the idea of providing well-designed, functional furniture at low prices, making good design accessible to everyone. The company's success hinges on its ability to deliver value through a unique combination of design, functionality, and affordability.

Key Strategies:

Flat-Pack Design: IKEA's innovative flat-pack furniture, designed for easy transport and self-assembly, addresses both cost-efficiency and customer convenience, reducing shipping and storage costs.

Product Design and Functionality: The company invests heavily in product design, ensuring that its furniture is not only stylish but also functional and suited to a wide range of living situations. This focus on design and functionality meets the consumer's desire for products that fit their lifestyle and budget.

Cost-Efficiency: IKEA's cost-conscious manufacturing processes, including the use of sustainable and less expensive materials, allow it to price its products competitively, making stylish home furnishings accessible to a broader market.

Impact:

IKEA's application of the product concept has revolutionized the furniture industry by demonstrating that it is possible to offer quality and design at low prices. The company's approach has not only met consumer desires for affordable yet stylish home furnishings but has also set new standards for the industry in terms of product design, sustainability, and value for money.

Patagonia and Societal Marketing

Patagonia's marketing approach exemplifies the societal marketing concept, which holds that companies should make good marketing decisions by considering consumers' wants, the company's requirements, and society's long-term interests. Patagonia's commitment to environmental sustainability and ethical practices has positioned it as a leader in societal marketing, appealing to a demographic that values social responsibility alongside product quality.

Key Strategies:

Environmental Activism: Patagonia has been at the forefront of environmental activism, donating a portion of its profits to conservation efforts and engaging in campaigns to protect natural habitats.

Sustainable Products: The company is committed to using recycled materials and organic cotton, reducing its carbon footprint, and encouraging customers to buy less and choose durable products.

Transparency: Patagonia's marketing includes transparent communication about its supply chain, labor practices, and environmental impact, building trust with consumers who value honesty and ethical practices.

Impact:

Patagonia's dedication to societal marketing has not only bolstered its brand image but has also inspired a loyal customer base that shares the company's environmental values. By integrating its commitment to sustainability into every aspect of its operations and marketing, Patagonia has set a benchmark for ethical business practices, proving that companies can be successful while making a positive impact on society.

Zappos and Relationship Marketing

Zappos, an online shoe and clothing retailer, is renowned for its exceptional customer service and commitment to customer satisfaction, making it a paragon of relationship marketing. This marketing approach focuses on building long-term relationships with customers, emphasizing customer loyalty, satisfaction, and engagement.

Key Strategies:

Exceptional Customer Service: Zappos offers a 365-day return policy, free shipping both ways, and a call center that is open 24/7, ensuring that customer service is always a top priority.

Company Culture: Zappos has cultivated a company culture centered around customer happiness and empowerment of employees to go the extra mile for customers, leading to positive customer experiences.

Engagement and Personalization: Through personalized marketing and engagement strategies, including targeted emails and a strong social media presence, Zappos fosters a sense of community and connection with its brand.

Impact:

Zappos' focus on relationship marketing has resulted in high levels of customer loyalty and repeat business, distinguishing it in the competitive e-commerce space. By prioritizing customer satisfaction and building strong relationships, Zappos has achieved remarkable success and has become a model for customer service excellence.

Each of these case studies demonstrates how foundational marketing theories can be applied in practice to drive business success. IKEA, Patagonia, and Zappos have each taken different marketing concepts and integrated them into their operations and strategies, showcasing the versatility and power of marketing to meet consumer needs, achieve societal goals, and build lasting relationships.

CHAPTER 3. THE SCIENCE OF MARKET RESEARCH

Market research stands as the backbone of informed decision-making in the business world, a disciplined approach to gathering, analyzing, and interpreting information that informs an organization's marketing strategy. This chapter delves into the science behind market research, unraveling the methodologies, best practices, and innovative tools that underpin this critical business function. It explores the diverse approaches to collecting and analyzing data, ensuring that businesses can navigate the complexities of consumer behavior and competitive landscapes with precision and insight.

The exploration begins with an overview of the diverse approaches to market research, distinguishing between quantitative and qualitative methodologies and introducing the benefits of a mixed-methods approach. This section sets the stage for understanding the broad spectrum of tools available to marketers, from surveys and focus groups to advanced analytics and social media monitoring.

Best practices in conducting market research are then examined, providing a roadmap for executing research projects that yield reliable and actionable insights. This includes formulating clear research objectives, selecting appropriate methodologies, ensuring representative sampling, maintaining objectivity, and accurately analyzing and interpreting data. These practices form the foundation of rigorous market research, ensuring that the insights derived are both valid and valuable for strategic decision-making.

The chapter progresses to unveil the innovative tools in market research, highlighting how technological advancements have transformed the way businesses gather and analyze data. From big data analytics to AI and machine learning, these tools offer unprecedented opportunities to mine deeper insights from both structured and unstructured data sources. The implications of these innovations for market research are profound, enabling more nuanced understanding of consumer behaviors and preferences.

Finally, market research across industries illustrates the application and significance of market research in different sectors, underscoring its versatility and critical role in driving industry-specific strategies. Whether in consumer goods, technology, healthcare, or services, market research provides the empirical evidence needed to make informed strategic decisions, tailor products and services to customer needs, and stay ahead in a competitive marketplace.

Through a detailed exploration of the science of market research, this chapter equips readers with the knowledge and tools to harness the power of data-driven insights. It emphasizes the strategic importance of market research in understanding consumers, optimizing products and services, and navigating the ever-changing business environment. As the marketplace becomes increasingly complex and competitive, the role of market research as a key driver of business success has never been more critical.

3.1 DIVERSE APPROACHES TO MARKET RESEARCH

Market research encompasses a range of methodologies designed to gather information about consumers' needs, preferences, behaviors, and perceptions. These methodologies fall into two primary categories: quantitative and qualitative research.

Quantitative Research involves collecting numerical data that can be quantified and subjected to statistical analysis. Common techniques include surveys, questionnaires, and structured interviews, providing insights into market size, consumer preferences, and buying patterns.

Surveys and Questionnaires: Tools like SurveyMonkey or Google Forms enable the collection of large datasets from diverse audiences. For example, McDonald's might use online surveys to gauge customer satisfaction with their menu across different regions.

Structured Interviews: Conducting telephone or face-to-face interviews to collect numerical data. A tech company like Samsung could use structured interviews to assess customer satisfaction with its latest smartphone model.

Qualitative Research, on the other hand, focuses on understanding the 'why' behind consumer choices and behaviors. It employs methods such as focus groups, in-depth interviews, and participant observation to gather non-numerical data. This type of research is invaluable for exploring attitudes, feelings, and motivations.

Focus Groups: Gathering a small group of people to discuss a product or concept in depth. Dove's "Real Beauty" campaign might have used focus group feedback to understand women's perceptions of beauty industry standards.

Ethnographic Research: Observing consumers in their natural environment. IKEA could employ ethnographic research to understand how customers interact with furniture in their homes, leading to the design of more functional products.

Mixed-Methods Research combines both quantitative and qualitative approaches, providing a comprehensive view of the market. This approach allows researchers to validate quantitative data with qualitative insights, offering a deeper understanding of the research subject.

3.2 BEST PRACTICES IN CONDUCTING MARKET RESEARCH

Conducting effective market research requires adherence to several best practices to ensure the reliability and usefulness of the findings.

Define the Research Objectives: Clearly defining what you aim to discover through your research is crucial. This helps in selecting the appropriate methodology and focusing the research efforts.

Choose the Right Methodology: Selecting the appropriate research methodology, whether quantitative, qualitative, or mixed-methods, depends on the research objectives and the type of information needed.

Ensure Representative Sampling: The sample chosen for research should accurately represent the broader population to ensure the findings are applicable and reliable.

Maintain Objectivity: Researchers must remain unbiased and objective, avoiding leading questions that could influence respondents' answers.

Analyze and Interpret Data Accurately: Collecting data is just the beginning; interpreting it accurately to draw meaningful insights is critical for informing business strategies.

3.3 INNOVATIVE TOOLS IN MARKET RESEARCH

Technological advancements have introduced a plethora of innovative tools that enhance the efficiency and effectiveness of market research.

Big Data Analytics allows for the analysis of vast datasets to identify patterns, trends, and insights that were previously unattainable.

Social Media Listening Tools enable researchers to monitor conversations and sentiments expressed online, providing real-time insights into consumer attitudes and behaviors.

Mobile Surveys and Apps facilitate the collection of data in real-time, reaching respondents across diverse geographies and demographics.

AI and Machine Learning technologies are increasingly being used to analyze qualitative data, identifying themes and sentiments in large volumes of text.

3.4 MARKET RESEARCH ACROSS INDUSTRIES

Market research is a foundational element across various industries, enabling businesses to understand consumer needs, market trends, competitive landscapes, and emerging opportunities. The application and focus of market research can vary significantly from one industry to another, reflecting unique challenges and opportunities inherent to each sector. Here's an exploration of how market research is applied across different industries, highlighting its critical role in informing strategic decisions.

Consumer Goods Industry

In the consumer goods sector, market research is pivotal for understanding consumer preferences, product performance, and brand positioning. Companies frequently conduct surveys, focus groups, and product testing to gauge consumer reactions to new products or variations. For example, a food and beverage company might use taste tests and consumer surveys to determine the preferred flavors in a new line of products before launching them to the market. This direct feedback loop helps in tailoring products to meet consumer tastes and increasing the likelihood of market success.

Case Study: P&G's "Connect + Develop" Program

P&G, a global leader in consumer goods, has revolutionized its approach to innovation through its "Connect + Develop" program. This initiative involves using market research not only to understand consumer needs but also to identify and collaborate with external partners, including startups, inventors, and other companies, to bring new ideas to market. An example of this is the development of the Swiffer, a now-iconic cleaning product that was born from a collaboration with an external inventor. Market research identified a need for easier, more efficient cleaning solutions, leading P&G to partner with the inventor who had developed a unique cleaning technology.

Technology and Electronics Industry

The fast-paced nature of the technology and electronics industry makes market research crucial for staying ahead of trends and innovation cycles. Companies in this sector often focus on usability studies, customer satisfaction research, and trend analysis to inform product development and marketing strategies. For instance, a smartphone manufacturer might analyze consumer usage patterns and feature preferences to design its next model, ensuring it meets evolving consumer demands and stays competitive in the market.

Case Study: Apple's Product Development Strategy

Apple's success with products like the iPhone and MacBook is partly attributed to its rigorous market research process. Before launching the first iPhone, Apple conducted extensive research to understand consumer frustrations with existing smartphones and feature phones. Insights into consumers' desires for a more intuitive user interface, better internet browsing capabilities, and a more seamless integration of music, phone, and internet functionalities guided the development of the iPhone, a product that revolutionized the smartphone industry.

Healthcare and Pharmaceuticals

Market research in healthcare and pharmaceuticals is essential for understanding patient needs, treatment outcomes, and market potential for new drugs or medical devices. Beyond traditional consumer research, this industry also relies on clinical trials, regulatory research, and health economics outcomes research (HEOR) to guide product development and market entry strategies. For example, a pharmaceutical company developing a new medication for diabetes must not only understand the medical efficacy of its product but also patients' and healthcare providers' perspectives on usability, side effects, and pricing considerations.

Case Study: Pfizer and Patient-Centric Drug Development

Pfizer, one of the world's largest pharmaceutical companies, has increasingly focused on patient-centric market research to guide the development of new medications. For the development of a new breast cancer drug, Pfizer conducted in-depth research with patients to understand their treatment experiences, concerns, and desired outcomes. This patient-centric approach ensured that the final product not only addressed the clinical aspects of breast cancer but also aligned with patients' preferences and quality-of-life considerations.

Retail Industry

In retail, market research helps companies understand shopping behaviors, preferences, and the effectiveness of various sales channels. Retailers use customer satisfaction surveys, foot traffic analysis, and online shopping behavior studies to optimize store layouts, product assortments, and e-commerce platforms. For instance, a clothing retailer might analyze the impact of in-store displays on purchase behavior or use online shopping data to personalize marketing messages and promotions to individual customers.

Case Study: Target's Omnichannel Strategy

Target has successfully used market research to enhance its omnichannel retail strategy, ensuring a seamless customer experience across online and in-store channels. Research identified a growing consumer demand for convenience and flexibility in shopping. In response, Target implemented services like curbside pickup and same-day delivery, which were heavily informed by insights into customers' shopping behaviors and preferences. This omnichannel approach has helped Target increase customer satisfaction and loyalty.

Financial Services

The financial services industry uses market research to gauge consumer attitudes towards different financial products, brand trust, and service satisfaction levels. This information can inform product development, such as creating more user-friendly mobile banking apps, or marketing strategies that address consumer pain points with existing services. For example, a bank might conduct market research to understand the features most desired by its customers in a mobile banking app, such as security, ease of use, or real-time notifications.

Case Study: Bank of America's Mobile Banking Enhancements

Bank of America has utilized market research to continuously improve its mobile banking services. Understanding the importance of mobile banking for younger consumers, the bank conducted research to identify the most desired features and functionalities in a banking app. Insights led to the introduction of features like mobile check deposit and personalized financial insights, significantly improving user satisfaction and engagement with the app.

Entertainment and Media

In the entertainment and media industry, market research is used to understand audience preferences, consumption patterns, and content trends. Streaming services, for example, analyze viewer data to recommend personalized content and inform future content creation decisions. A streaming platform might use viewer feedback and viewership data to decide which shows to renew, which genres to invest in more heavily, and how to market new releases to maximize engagement.

Case Study: Netflix's Content Strategy

Netflix employs sophisticated data analytics and market research to inform its content creation and acquisition strategies. By analyzing viewership data, consumer preferences, and viewing patterns, Netflix identifies genres and themes that are likely to perform well. This approach informed decisions to produce hit series like "Stranger Things" and "The Crown," which were developed in response to identified gaps in the entertainment market and have contributed significantly to Netflix's success.

CHAPTER 4. DECODING CONSUMER BEHAVIOR

Decoding consumer behavior is akin to unlocking a vast and complex puzzle where each piece represents different influences, motivations, and decisions that drive consumers towards their purchasing choices. This chapter embarks on a comprehensive journey through the intricate world of consumer behavior, exploring the psychological underpinnings, social factors, personal characteristics, and external influences that collectively shape how consumers interact with the market

Beginning with an exploration of consumer psychology, we delve into the cognitive processes that guide how individuals perceive, interpret, and react to marketing messages. This section illuminates the subtle yet powerful ways in which marketers can align their strategies with the psychological needs and desires of their target audience.

The discussion then shifts to the impact of social factors, recognizing the pivotal role of family, friends, social networks, and cultural norms in shaping buying behaviors. Here, we examine how social media and influencer marketing have become indispensable tools for marketers aiming to leverage social proof and community influence.

In understanding consumer personalities and lifestyles, we acknowledge the diversity of consumer preferences and how personal identity and lifestyle choices drive brand loyalty and product selection. This segment highlights the importance of targeted marketing in appealing to specific lifestyle segments.

The consumer decision-making process is dissected to reveal the stages consumers navigate from recognizing a need to making a purchase and reflecting on their decision. This process underscores the opportunities for marketers to engage and influence consumers at each step.

We further explore the role of emotions in consumer choices, showcasing how brands like Coca-Cola create emotional connections that transcend the functional benefits of their products, fostering loyalty and affection towards the brand.

The principles of behavioral economics offer insights into the irrationalities and biases that affect consumer decisions, providing strategies for marketers to design offers and experiences that resonate with these unconscious influences.

Addressing cultural influences and global consumer behavior, this section highlights the challenges and strategies for brands operating in diverse international markets, emphasizing the need for cultural sensitivity and adaptation.

The transformative influence of technology and digital environments on consumer behavior is examined, with a focus on how digital platforms, AI, and personalization have reshaped the way consumers discover, evaluate, and purchase products.

Sustainable consumer behavior reflects a growing segment of the market where environmental and ethical considerations influence buying decisions. Brands that align with these values, like Adidas, are showcased as leaders in leveraging sustainability as a competitive advantage.

Finally, the chapter concludes with strategies for adapting marketing strategies to consumer behavior, demonstrating how businesses can thrive by being attuned to the evolving preferences, behaviors, and values of their consumers.

Through real-life examples and in-depth analysis, this chapter provides marketers with the insights and tools necessary to understand and influence consumer behavior effectively. It's a guide to crafting marketing strategies that are not only effective but also resonate deeply with the values, needs, and desires of the consumer base.

4.1 UNDERSTANDING CONSUMER PSYCHOLOGY

Consumer psychology delves into the cognitive, emotional, and social processes that influence individuals' purchasing decisions. It's a field that bridges psychology and marketing, offering insights into how consumers perceive products, brands, and their own needs. Understanding consumer psychology is crucial for marketers aiming to craft messages and products that resonate deeply with their target audience.

The Role of Perception and Attitude

Perception and attitude play pivotal roles in consumer psychology. How a consumer perceives a product can significantly influence their attitude towards it and, consequently, their purchasing decision. For example, Apple has mastered the art of creating a positive perception through sleek design and branding, which fosters a positive attitude towards its products, even before consumers assess the technical specifications.

Motivation and Needs

Consumer psychology also explores the motivations behind consumer purchases, often drawing on Maslow's Hierarchy of Needs. A classic illustration is the marketing strategies of luxury brands like Rolex or Louis Vuitton, which appeal to consumers' desires for esteem and self-actualization, beyond just the functional value of the products.

Decision-Making Processes

The decision-making process is another critical aspect of consumer psychology. It involves several stages, from problem recognition and information search to the evaluation of alternatives and the final purchase decision. Understanding these stages allows marketers to present information and options tailored to influence the consumer at each point effectively. Amazon, for example, utilizes customer data to recommend products, simplifying the information search and evaluation process for its users.

The Power of Emotions

Emotions significantly influence consumer behavior. Brands that can evoke emotions through their marketing campaigns often see a stronger consumer connection to their products. Dove's "Real Beauty" campaign is a prime example, where the brand used real stories of women to evoke feelings of empowerment and self-confidence, strengthening consumers' emotional connection to Dove.

Social Influence

The impact of social influence on consumer behavior is profound. Consumers are often swayed by the opinions, behaviors, and endorsements of others, particularly in today's digital age where social media influencers play a significant role. The success of influencer marketing campaigns, such as those by Fashion Nova, relies on the psychological principle that people tend to conform to perceived social norms and behaviors admired by those they follow.

Cognitive Dissonance

After making a purchase, consumers may experience cognitive dissonance, especially if the product does not meet their expectations or if they are presented with information that conflicts with their purchase decision. Brands often try to minimize dissonance through satisfaction guarantees and return policies, aiming to maintain a positive brand perception. Zappos, with its customer-friendly return policy, effectively addresses cognitive dissonance, ensuring customers feel confident and satisfied with their purchases.

Understanding consumer psychology is foundational for creating marketing strategies that not only attract attention but also resonate on a deeper level, leading to lasting brand loyalty and consumer satisfaction. By tapping into the psychological underpinnings of consumer behavior, marketers can design more effective, empathetic, and engaging marketing campaigns.

4.2 THE IMPACT OF SOCIAL FACTORS

Social factors play a crucial role in shaping consumer behavior, influencing everything from the products we buy to the brands we prefer and the shopping habits we exhibit. These factors include family, social networks, cultural norms, and the broader societal context in which consumers live and make purchasing decisions. Understanding the impact of these social factors is vital for marketers aiming to connect more deeply with their target audiences.

Family Influence

The family unit is often the first social group that influences consumer behavior. Purchasing habits, brand preferences, and even attitudes toward spending can be rooted in family traditions and values. For instance, a household that prioritizes sustainability may influence its members to choose eco-friendly brands like Patagonia, which aligns with their environmental values. Marketers targeting products for the home or family use often craft messages that appeal to shared values and collective decision-making processes.

Reference Groups and Social Networks

Reference groups, including friends, colleagues, and social networks, significantly impact consumer choices. People are influenced by their peers' opinions and behaviors, seeking their approval and often conforming to group norms. Social media platforms have amplified this effect, where a recommendation from a peer or an influencer can sway purchasing decisions. Brands like Glossier have leveraged social networks effectively, using user-generated content and influencer partnerships to build trust and authenticity around their products.

Cultural Norms and Values

Culture shapes consumers' perceptions, beliefs, and behaviors, influencing their buying habits. Marketers must understand cultural nuances to avoid missteps and to resonate with consumers in diverse markets. For example, McDonald's adapts its menu to local tastes and cultural preferences in different countries, offering vegetarian options in India and halal food in Middle Eastern markets, demonstrating sensitivity to cultural norms.

Social Class

Social class, determined by factors such as income, education, and occupation, also affects consumer behavior. Luxury brands, for instance, target upper social classes with high-end products and exclusive marketing messages that convey status and prestige. In contrast, value-oriented brands like Walmart focus on affordability and accessibility, appealing to a broader base seeking quality and value.

Social Trends and Movements

Consumer behavior is also influenced by broader social trends and movements. The growing awareness of environmental issues and social justice has led to an increase in demand for sustainable and ethically produced products. Brands that align themselves with these movements, such as Ben & Jerry's with its commitment to social activism, can strengthen their connection with consumers who share these values.

The Role of Social Media

Social media has transformed the way consumers interact with brands and each other, offering a platform for sharing opinions, experiences, and recommendations. The viral nature of social media content means that consumer perceptions and trends can change rapidly, requiring brands to stay engaged and responsive. Nike's use of social media to promote inclusivity and diversity in sports, for example, has helped the brand maintain its relevance and appeal among younger, socially conscious consumers.

Understanding the impact of social factors requires marketers to look beyond individual consumer behavior and consider the broader social context. By recognizing the influence of family, social networks, culture, and societal trends, brands can tailor their marketing strategies to resonate more deeply with their target audience, fostering loyalty and driving purchasing decisions.

4.3 CONSUMER PERSONALITIES AND LIFESTYLES

The intricacies of consumer personalities and lifestyles are pivotal in shaping their preferences, purchasing behaviors, and brand interactions. These aspects of consumer identity not only influence individual choices but also dictate the broader trends within the market. By understanding the diverse personalities and lifestyles of their target audience, marketers can craft strategies that resonate on a personal level, fostering a deeper connection and loyalty.

Understanding Consumer Personalities

Consumer personality refers to the psychological traits that influence an individual's buying behavior. The Big Five personality traits—openness, conscientiousness, extraversion, agreeableness, and neuroticism—offer a framework for understanding these influences. For instance, individuals high in openness may be more inclined towards innovative and novel products, while those high in conscientiousness might prefer products known for reliability and value. Luxury brands like Mercedes-Benz, known for their emphasis on quality and prestige, appeal particularly to those with high conscientiousness, showcasing how personality traits can guide marketing strategies.

Lifestyles and Buying Behavior

Lifestyles represent the combination of activities, interests, and opinions that define how a person spends their time and what they value. Lifestyle segmentation involves categorizing consumers based on shared traits, which can significantly enhance the effectiveness of targeted marketing campaigns. For example, a brand like Lululemon targets consumers leading an active, health-conscious lifestyle, using marketing messages that emphasize wellness, community, and personal growth.

Tailoring Marketing to Personalities and Lifestyles

The key to leveraging consumer personalities and lifestyles in marketing lies in the ability to tailor messages and product offerings to meet the specific needs and desires of different segments. Spotify's personalized playlists and recommendations serve as an excellent example of this approach, catering to the individual's music preferences, mood, and listening habits, which are intrinsic to their lifestyle and personality.

Case Study: GoPro and Adventure Seekers

GoPro targets consumers with a strong inclination towards adventure and excitement. By focusing on this specific lifestyle, GoPro positions its cameras as essential tools for capturing extraordinary moments, whether it's skydiving, surfing, or mountain biking. The brand's marketing strategy utilizes user-generated content to showcase real-life experiences, resonating with consumers who value adventure, authenticity, and self-expression.

The Role of Psychographics in Marketing

Psychographics go beyond basic demographics to include psychological attributes, providing a richer understanding of consumer personalities and lifestyles. This approach allows for more nuanced marketing strategies that address the motivations, concerns, and aspirations of different consumer segments. For instance, Tesla's marketing appeals to environmentally conscious consumers who prioritize sustainability, innovation, and cutting-edge technology, aligning with their lifestyle and values.

Digital Lifestyles and E-Commerce

The rise of digital lifestyles has transformed consumer behavior, with a significant shift towards online shopping, digital entertainment, and social media engagement. E-commerce platforms like Amazon have capitalized on this shift by offering convenience, variety, and personalized shopping experiences, catering to the digital lifestyle and its demand for efficiency and instant gratification.

4.4 CONSUMER DECISION-MAKING PROCESS

The consumer decision-making process is a complex journey that involves a series of steps leading from recognizing a need to making a purchase and reflecting on that decision post-purchase. Understanding this process is crucial for marketers to effectively guide consumers towards their products and services at each stage, ultimately influencing their final purchasing decisions.

Stages of the Consumer Decision-Making Process

Problem Recognition: The process begins when consumers recognize a need or a problem that requires a solution. This could be triggered by internal stimuli (e.g., hunger leading to the purchase of food) or external stimuli (e.g., seeing an advertisement for a new pair of shoes).

Real-Life Example: Nike creates awareness for its latest running shoes through targeted advertising, triggering problem recognition among consumers who might be looking for high-quality athletic footwear.

Information Search: Once a need is recognized, consumers seek information to make an informed decision. This search can be internal, based on past experiences, or external, involving friends, family, online reviews, and company websites.

Real-Life Example: Before purchasing a smartphone, a consumer might visit tech review sites like CNET or TechRadar, seek opinions on social media, or ask friends for recommendations.

Evaluation of Alternatives: Consumers compare different products or brands based on criteria important to them, such as price, quality, features, and brand reputation. This stage is crucial as it determines the set of options from which the consumer will make their final choice.

Real-Life Example: A consumer deciding between a Tesla Model 3 and a Chevrolet Bolt will weigh factors such as price, range, features, and brand perception.

Purchase Decision: The consumer selects their preferred product or service and makes the purchase. However, this decision can still be influenced by factors such as promotional offers, financing options, or last-minute doubts.

Real-Life Example: Apple Stores and their website streamline the purchase process for an iPhone with easy navigation, clear pricing, and financing options, reducing friction at this critical stage.

Post-Purchase Behavior: After the purchase, consumers evaluate their decision based on the product's performance relative to their expectations. Satisfaction or dissatisfaction at this stage can influence repeat purchases and word-of-mouth recommendations.

Real-Life Example: Amazon follows up on purchases with emails inviting customers to review their bought items, addressing post-purchase evaluation and potentially influencing future buying behavior.

Influencing the Decision-Making Process

Marketers can influence each stage of the decision-making process through targeted strategies. For example, during the problem recognition stage, creating content that highlights common problems solved by the product can awaken a need. In the information search and evaluation stages, providing detailed product information, comparisons, testimonials, and reviews can guide the consumer towards the brand. Special promotions and assurances like money-back guarantees can tip the scales in favor of purchase decisions. Finally, ensuring product quality and excellent customer service helps secure positive post-purchase evaluations, fostering brand loyalty and advocacy.

The Role of Cognitive Biases

Cognitive biases, such as the anchoring effect or confirmation bias, can also influence the decision-making process. Marketers must be aware of these biases to craft messages that resonate with consumers' subconscious inclinations. For example, presenting a high-priced item before showing a moderately priced one can make the latter seem more appealing—a tactic often used in pricing strategies.

4.5 THE ROLE OF EMOTIONS IN CONSUMER CHOICES

The influence of emotions on consumer choices is a powerful and often decisive factor in the purchasing process. Emotional connections can surpass logical evaluations, leading consumers to choose products that evoke positive feelings or align with their self-image and values. Understanding the role of emotions in consumer behavior is crucial for marketers aiming to create compelling, resonant messages that drive engagement and loyalty.

Emotional Branding and Consumer Loyalty

Emotional branding seeks to build relationships between a brand and its consumers by appealing to the latter's emotional needs and desires. This approach aims to create a loyal customer base by associating products with specific feelings or experiences. For instance, Coca-Cola's "Open Happiness" campaign successfully associated the brand with feelings of joy, community, and nostalgia, transcending the physical product to sell an experience.

The Impact of Positive and Negative Emotions

Positive emotions, such as happiness, love, and trust, can significantly enhance brand perception and loyalty. Consumers are more likely to remember and choose brands that have made them feel good in the past. Conversely, negative emotions, like frustration or disappointment with a product or service, can lead to negative word-of-mouth and a loss of trust in the brand. Apple's focus on creating intuitive, user-friendly products aims to minimize frustration and enhance satisfaction, fostering positive brand associations.

Emotional Decision-Making in Advertising

Advertisements that evoke strong emotional reactions are more likely to be remembered and shared. By tapping into universal emotions, brands can create ads that resonate across diverse audiences. For example, Nike's "Just

Do It" campaign inspires motivation and determination, appealing to consumers' aspirations and emotional desires to be their best selves.

The Role of Storytelling

Storytelling is a powerful tool for emotional engagement, allowing brands to communicate their values and build a deeper connection with consumers. Stories that reflect consumers' experiences, hopes, and dreams can be particularly effective. Dove's "Real Beauty" campaign uses storytelling to challenge beauty standards, fostering an emotional bond with consumers who identify with the message of self-acceptance and empowerment.

Consumer Psychology and Emotional Triggers

Understanding consumer psychology is key to identifying the emotional triggers that can influence purchasing decisions. These triggers can be deeply personal and vary widely among individuals, but common themes include the desire for security, belonging, self-esteem, and achievement. Luxury brands, such as Rolex, trigger emotions related to status and achievement, while safety-oriented brands like Volvo appeal to the need for security and protection.

Social Media and Emotional Engagement

Social media platforms have become critical arenas for emotional engagement, offering brands opportunities to interact with consumers in real-time and foster emotional connections. Through comments, likes, and shares, consumers express their feelings about brands and products, influencing others in their networks. Emotional engagement on social media can amplify positive brand experiences and mitigate negative ones, as seen in how brands like Starbucks use their platforms to engage with customers, celebrate their stories, and address concerns.

4.6 BEHAVIORAL ECONOMICS AND CONSUMER BEHAVIOR

Behavioral economics bridges the gap between psychology and economic decision-making, providing insights into how emotional, social, and cognitive factors influence the choices consumers make. Unlike traditional economic theory, which assumes rational decision-making, behavioral economics recognizes that consumers often act irrationally due to various biases and heuristics. Understanding these principles can help marketers design more effective strategies by aligning with or gently nudging against consumers' natural tendencies.

Key Principles of Behavioral Economics Influencing Consumer Behavior

Loss Aversion: People tend to prefer avoiding losses over acquiring equivalent gains. For example, a marketing campaign that emphasizes what consumers stand to lose by not using a product (e.g., "Don't miss out on this opportunity") can be more persuasive than one that highlights potential gains.

The Decoy Effect: When given two options, consumers can struggle to decide. However, adding a third, less attractive option (the decoy) can make one of the original options more appealing. A classic case is subscription models where a premium option makes the mid-tier option look more valuable.

Anchoring: This occurs when individuals rely too heavily on the first piece of information offered (the "anchor") when making decisions. Retailers use this by showing the "original" price alongside the sale price, making the discount seem more significant.

The Endowment Effect: Consumers value an item more highly once they own it. Free trials exploit this effect by giving consumers ownership of a product for a limited time, making them more likely to purchase it because they've become accustomed to its benefits.

Social Proof: People are influenced by the actions and approvals of others. Online reviews and testimonials leverage social proof, suggesting that because others are satisfied with a product or service, it must be worthwhile.

Applying Behavioral Economics in Marketing

Creating Urgency with Limited-Time Offers: By emphasizing the scarcity and time sensitivity of an offer, marketers can tap into consumers' fear of missing out (FOMO) and loss aversion, encouraging quicker decision-making.

Price Perception Strategies: Introducing a high-priced "anchor" product can make other options seem more reasonably priced. Luxury brands often employ this strategy, offering ultra-premium products to make their entry-level luxury items appear more accessible.

Leveraging Social Proof: Brands like Amazon display customer reviews prominently, knowing that positive feedback from other consumers significantly influences purchasing decisions.

Subscription Models and the Endowment Effect: Services like Spotify and Netflix offer free or discounted trial periods, betting that once consumers experience the full benefits of the service, they will be reluctant to give them up, leading to paid subscriptions.

Behavioral Economics in Digital Marketing

Digital platforms offer unique opportunities to apply behavioral economics principles through personalized marketing and A/B testing. By analyzing consumer data, digital marketers can identify which biases influence their target audience's decision-making and tailor their strategies accordingly. For instance, personalization algorithms can present products similar to those the consumer has shown interest in, leveraging the familiarity bias.

4.7 CULTURAL INFLUENCES AND GLOBAL CONSUMER BEHAVIOR

Cultural influences play a pivotal role in shaping consumer behavior across the globe. Culture encompasses the shared values, beliefs, norms, and practices of a group of people, deeply influencing their purchasing decisions, brand perceptions, and consumption habits. For marketers operating in a global marketplace, understanding and adapting to these cultural nuances is crucial for success. It ensures that marketing strategies are not only effective but also respectful and relevant to diverse audiences.

Understanding Cultural Dimensions

Geert Hofstede's cultural dimensions theory provides a framework for understanding the impacts of a society's culture on the values of its members and how these values relate to behavior. Key dimensions include individualism vs. collectivism, uncertainty avoidance, power distance, masculinity vs. femininity, and long-term vs. short-term orientation. For example, in individualistic cultures (like the United States), marketing messages emphasizing personal achievement and freedom tend to resonate more. In contrast, in collectivist cultures (such as Japan), messages highlighting community and family align better with societal values.

The Role of Language and Symbols

Language and symbols carry deep cultural meanings that can significantly impact the effectiveness of marketing communications. For instance, color symbolism varies greatly between cultures: white is traditionally associated with purity in Western cultures but with mourning in many Eastern cultures. Similarly, certain phrases or slogans might not translate well across languages, leading to misunderstandings or even offense. Brands like KFC and Pepsi have learned this the hard way, with slogans translating into unintended meanings in other languages.

Cultural Adaptation in Global Marketing

Successful global brands often adapt their products, messaging, and marketing strategies to align with local cultures. McDonald's offers menu items tailored to local tastes, such as the McArabia in Middle Eastern countries or the Teriyaki Burger in Japan, reflecting the importance of cultural adaptation in product offerings. Similarly, global advertising campaigns are often localized to reflect local languages, values, and humor, ensuring that they resonate with each specific audience.

Case Study: Coca-Cola's Global Marketing Strategy

Coca-Cola is a prime example of a brand that effectively adapts its marketing strategies to cultural nuances. While maintaining a consistent brand image worldwide, Coca-Cola tailors its advertisements and community initiatives to reflect local cultures, celebrations, and values. This approach not only enhances the brand's global appeal but also strengthens its local market presence.

Consumer Ethnocentrism and Global Brands

Consumer ethnocentrism, the belief that purchasing foreign-made products is unpatriotic or wrong, can pose challenges for global brands. Marketers must navigate these sentiments by emphasizing the local benefits of their global brand, such as job creation or community involvement, or by incorporating local elements into their products and marketing efforts.

Digital Culture and Global Consumer Behavior

The rise of digital culture has also influenced global consumer behavior, creating a new layer of cultural influence that transcends traditional geographical boundaries. Social media platforms, for example, have fostered global trends and communities, allowing brands to engage with a worldwide audience more easily. However, the digital divide and varying levels of access to technology across different regions still necessitate a nuanced approach to digital marketing strategies.

4.8 THE INFLUENCE OF TECHNOLOGY AND DIGITAL ENVIRONMENTS

The influence of technology and digital environments on consumer behavior is profound and far-reaching, reshaping how consumers discover, evaluate, and purchase products and services. The digital revolution has not only transformed the marketplace but also the way brands interact with their consumers. From social media platforms to artificial intelligence and mobile commerce, technology has created new opportunities and challenges for marketers aiming to capture the attention and loyalty of digitally savvy consumers.

E-commerce and Online Shopping

The rise of e-commerce has dramatically changed consumer purchasing habits, offering convenience, wider selection, and often better pricing than traditional retail. Platforms like Amazon and Alibaba have set new standards in consumer expectations for ease of purchase, delivery speed, and customer service. This shift has compelled brick-and-mortar retailers to adopt omnichannel strategies, integrating their online and offline experiences to meet consumer demands.

Personalization and Data Analytics

Advancements in data analytics and machine learning have enabled unprecedented levels of personalization in marketing. By analyzing consumer data, companies can tailor their marketing messages, product recommendations, and even website experiences to individual preferences. Netflix's recommendation algorithm, which suggests content based on viewing history, is a prime example of personalization at scale, enhancing user satisfaction and engagement.

Social Media and Influencer Marketing

Social media platforms have transformed the way consumers interact with brands and each other, offering a space for sharing opinions, experiences, and product recommendations. Influencer marketing has emerged as a powerful strategy within this space, with brands leveraging the credibility and reach of social media personalities to influence consumer decisions. The success of beauty brands like Glossier, built largely on social media buzz and influencer partnerships, underscores the impact of these platforms on consumer behavior.

Mobile Commerce and Apps

The proliferation of smartphones has led to the rise of mobile commerce, with consumers increasingly making purchases directly from their mobile devices. Mobile apps offer a seamless shopping experience, with features like push notifications for promotions, easy payment systems, and location-based services enhancing consumer engagement. Starbucks' mobile app, which integrates payments, rewards, and ordering, exemplifies how brands can use mobile technology to enhance convenience and loyalty.

Virtual and Augmented Reality

Virtual and augmented reality (VR and AR) technologies are beginning to influence consumer behavior by offering immersive shopping experiences. IKEA's AR app, which allows consumers to visualize furniture in their homes before purchasing, demonstrates how these technologies can reduce uncertainty and improve customer satisfaction in the decision-making process.

The Impact of Digital Communities

Online communities, forums, and review sites play a significant role in shaping consumer opinions and decisions. Digital word-of-mouth through platforms like TripAdvisor and Yelp, as well as product review sections on e-commerce sites, significantly impact consumer trust and purchasing behavior, highlighting the importance of maintaining a positive online reputation.

Ethical Considerations and Digital Privacy

As technology enables deeper insights into consumer behavior, ethical considerations and concerns about digital privacy have come to the forefront. Consumers are increasingly aware of and concerned about how their data is collected, used, and protected. Transparent data practices and respect for consumer privacy can enhance trust and loyalty, while failures in this area can lead to backlash and regulatory scrutiny.

4.9 SUSTAINABLE CONSUMER BEHAVIOR

Sustainable consumer behavior reflects a growing segment of the market where environmental concerns, ethical considerations, and social responsibility influence purchasing decisions. As awareness of global challenges such as climate change, pollution, and social inequality increases, more consumers are choosing brands and products that not only meet their needs but also contribute to the well-being of the planet and society. This shift towards sustainability is reshaping marketing strategies, with brands increasingly highlighting their commitment to environmentally friendly practices, ethical sourcing, and social responsibility.

The Rise of the Conscious Consumer

Conscious consumers prioritize products that are eco-friendly, ethically produced, and socially responsible. They are willing to pay a premium for goods that align with their values, often researching a brand's sustainability practices before making a purchase. This shift has led to the popularity of brands like Patagonia, which is renowned for its environmental activism, sustainable product lines, and ethical business practices. Patagonia's "Worn Wear" program, which encourages repairing, sharing, and recycling garments, directly appeals to consumers' desires for sustainability and responsible consumption.

The Impact on Brand Loyalty and Perception

Sustainability can significantly enhance brand loyalty and perception. Brands that demonstrate genuine commitment to sustainable practices tend to enjoy a more positive image, greater customer loyalty, and often, a competitive edge. For instance, Adidas's initiative to manufacture shoes using recycled ocean plastic has not only addressed environmental concerns but also elevated the brand's image among eco-conscious consumers.

Marketing Strategies for Sustainable Brands

Marketing strategies for sustainable brands often focus on transparency and authenticity. Consumers are increasingly skeptical of "greenwashing" —

claims of environmental friendliness that are misleading or unsubstantiated. Thus, brands like Lush Cosmetics emphasize transparency in their sourcing and production processes, offering detailed information about ingredient origins and the environmental impact of their products. This openness fosters trust and credibility among consumers.

Digital Platforms and Sustainable Consumerism

Social media and digital platforms play a crucial role in promoting sustainable consumerism. They provide a space for brands to communicate their sustainability efforts and for consumers to share experiences and recommendations. Campaigns that leverage storytelling, showcasing the journey towards sustainability and the impact of consumers' choices, can be particularly effective. The #WhoMadeMyClothes movement, initiated by Fashion Revolution, utilizes social media to encourage transparency in the fashion industry, engaging consumers and brands in a dialogue about ethical fashion.

Challenges and Opportunities

While the trend towards sustainable consumer behavior presents opportunities, it also poses challenges. One major challenge is the perception of higher costs associated with sustainable products. Brands must navigate this by communicating the long-term value and benefits of sustainable choices, not just in terms of environmental impact but also regarding quality and cost-effectiveness over time.

Future Directions

The demand for sustainable products is expected to grow, driven by increasing environmental awareness and consumer activism. This trend presents an opportunity for innovation in product development, packaging, and supply chain management to meet the evolving needs of the market. Brands that can authentically integrate sustainability into their operations, products, and marketing strategies are likely to thrive in the future marketplace.

4.10 ADAPTING MARKETING STRATEGIES TO CONSUMER BEHAVIOR

Adapting marketing strategies to match consumer behavior is essential for businesses aiming to stay relevant and competitive in today's rapidly changing marketplace. As consumer preferences evolve, influenced by technological advancements, cultural shifts, and growing awareness around issues such as sustainability, marketers must be agile and responsive. By closely observing and understanding these shifts in behavior, companies can tailor their marketing efforts to better meet consumer needs and expectations, thereby enhancing engagement, loyalty, and ultimately, sales.

Integrating Consumer Insights into Product Development

Understanding consumer behavior is crucial not just for marketing existing products but also for guiding product development. Insights into what consumers need, how they use products, and what values they prioritize can lead to innovation that resonates with the target market. For instance, the rise in health consciousness has led food and beverage companies like PepsiCo to develop healthier product lines with reduced sugar, natural ingredients, and clear labeling.

Personalization and Customization

In an era of information overload, personalization has emerged as a key strategy in capturing consumer attention and fostering loyalty. Leveraging data analytics, companies can now offer personalized experiences, from customized product recommendations on e-commerce sites like Amazon to individualized email marketing campaigns. This approach not only improves the consumer experience but also increases the efficiency of marketing efforts by targeting consumers more accurately.

Omnichannel Marketing

The consumer journey is no longer linear, with multiple touchpoints spanning online and offline channels. An omnichannel marketing approach ensures a seamless consumer experience across all platforms, whether it's in-store, on a website, or through social media. Retailers like Target and Best Buy have excelled in integrating their online and offline presence, offering services like online order in-store pickup, which caters to consumers' desire for convenience and flexibility.

Leveraging Social Media and Influencer Partnerships

Social media continues to be a powerful tool in shaping consumer behavior, offering brands a platform to engage directly with their audience. Influencer partnerships can amplify this effect, leveraging the trust and credibility that influencers have with their followers. Beauty brands, including Anastasia Beverly Hills and Tarte Cosmetics, have successfully used influencer partnerships to launch new products and reach wider audiences.

Responding to the Demand for Sustainability

As consumers increasingly prioritize sustainability, brands are adapting their marketing strategies to highlight their environmental and ethical practices. This involves not just promoting sustainable products but also adopting more eco-friendly marketing practices, such as reducing packaging and using digital rather than physical promotional materials. Patagonia's marketing, which focuses on the brand's commitment to environmental activism, resonates with consumers who value sustainability, influencing their purchasing decisions.

Agile Marketing in a Digital Age

The digital age demands agility in marketing strategies, with consumer trends and behaviors changing at an unprecedented pace. Real-time data analysis and digital marketing tools enable brands to respond quickly to these changes, adjusting their strategies to maintain relevance and engagement. Netflix, for example, uses viewer data to not only recommend content but also to inform content creation, ensuring it meets viewer preferences and behaviors.

Ethical Considerations and Transparency

With growing consumer awareness and concern over privacy, data security, and ethical business practices, transparency has become a crucial element of marketing strategies. Brands that are open about their practices, actively protect consumer data, and communicate honestly about their products and services can build trust and loyalty. Transparency in marketing not only meets consumer expectations but also aligns with broader social and ethical standards.

CHAPTER 5. ETHICS AND SOCIAL RESPONSIBILITY IN MARKETING

In today's business landscape, ethics and social responsibility in marketing are not merely optional; they are essential components of a successful and sustainable brand strategy. This chapter delves into the critical role of ethical considerations and social responsibility in shaping marketing practices, reflecting a paradigm shift towards more conscientious business operations. As consumers become increasingly informed and concerned about the environmental, social, and ethical implications of their purchasing decisions, businesses are compelled to adopt marketing strategies that prioritize transparency, integrity, and a commitment to positive societal impact.

The imperative for ethical marketing arises from the need to build trust and credibility with consumers. In an era marked by information accessibility and digital connectivity, any discrepancy between a brand's message and its actions is quickly brought to light, potentially damaging reputation and consumer trust. Ethical marketing practices, therefore, encompass honesty in advertising, respect for consumer privacy, and a commitment to fairness and transparency. By adhering to these principles, companies not only mitigate the risk of public backlash and legal repercussions but also strengthen their brand reputation and consumer loyalty.

Beyond individual ethics, social responsibility in marketing reflects a brand's commitment to contributing positively to society and the environment. This involves integrating sustainable practices into business operations, supporting charitable causes, engaging in community development, and advocating for social and environmental issues. Such initiatives resonate with the growing segment of consumers who prioritize sustainability and ethical considerations in their purchasing choices, offering brands an opportunity to align with these values and differentiate themselves in a crowded marketplace.

The impact of ethical marketing and social responsibility extends beyond consumer satisfaction and brand loyalty, contributing to broader societal and environmental benefits. By promoting sustainable consumption patterns, advocating for social justice, and engaging in ethical business practices, companies play a crucial role in addressing global challenges such as climate change, inequality, and health and wellness.

This chapter explores the nuances of navigating the complex interplay between marketing objectives and ethical considerations, providing insights into how businesses can adopt and communicate ethical and socially responsible marketing strategies. Through a series of case studies and examples, it illustrates the tangible benefits of ethical marketing practices, not just for the companies that adopt them but for society as a whole. In doing so, it highlights the evolving expectations of both consumers and businesses in the 21st century, emphasizing that success in the modern marketplace requires a commitment to ethics and social responsibility at the core of marketing strategies.

5.1 ADVOCATING ETHICAL MARKETING PRACTICES

Advocating ethical marketing practices is fundamental in today's business world, where consumers are increasingly seeking transparency, honesty, and integrity from the brands they support. Ethical marketing encompasses a wide range of practices that ensure companies conduct their advertising and communications in a way that is fair, truthful, and respectful to consumers and society at large. This approach not only builds trust and loyalty among customers but also contributes to the brand's long-term success and reputation.

The Core of Ethical Marketing

At the heart of ethical marketing lies the commitment to honesty in all marketing communications. This means avoiding misleading advertisements, exaggerating product benefits, or making false claims. For instance, a brand that accurately represents the capabilities and limitations of its products fosters trust and credibility with its audience.

Transparency

Transparency is another critical aspect of ethical marketing, requiring brands to be open about their business practices, sourcing, and the impact of their products on the environment and society. This could involve sharing details about the sustainability of materials, the conditions under which products are manufactured, or the company's efforts to reduce its carbon footprint. Transparency not only satisfies the growing consumer demand for responsible business practices but also sets a brand apart in a competitive market.

Privacy and Data Protection

In the digital age, ethical marketing also extends to how companies collect, use, and protect consumer data. With increasing concerns over privacy and data security, brands must ensure they handle customer information responsibly, complying with regulations like the GDPR in the European Union and respecting consumers' privacy preferences. Clear, concise policies on data usage and consumer rights regarding their data are now expected by customers worldwide.

Addressing Consumer Vulnerabilities

Ethical marketing practices require companies to consider the vulnerabilities of certain consumer groups, such as children, the elderly, or those with specific health conditions, and ensure that their marketing strategies do not exploit these vulnerabilities. This involves being mindful of the content and placement of advertisements to avoid misleading or pressuring these sensitive audiences.

Combatting Greenwashing

As environmental concerns become more prominent, some companies might be tempted to engage in greenwashing — making false or exaggerated claims about the environmental benefits of their products. Ethical marketing demands accuracy and substantiation of such claims, ensuring that companies contribute genuinely to environmental sustainability rather than merely exploiting it as a marketing ploy.

Encouraging Industry Standards

Advocating ethical marketing practices also involves setting and promoting industry standards, encouraging peers and competitors to adopt similar practices. This collective effort can lead to a more trustworthy and sustainable marketplace, benefiting consumers, businesses, and the environment.

5.2 INTEGRATING SOCIAL RESPONSIBILITY IN MARKETING STRATEGIES

Integrating social responsibility into marketing strategies has become a pivotal element for brands aiming to connect with today's ethically conscious consumers. This approach not only demonstrates a company's commitment to making a positive impact on society and the environment but also resonates with consumers who prioritize sustainability, ethical production, and corporate responsibility in their purchasing decisions. The process involves embedding social, environmental, and ethical considerations into the core of marketing practices, thereby aligning brand values with consumer expectations for responsible business conduct.

Companies that successfully integrate social responsibility into their marketing strategies often see a boost in brand image, customer loyalty, and ultimately, business performance. This integration can take various forms, from leveraging marketing campaigns that highlight charitable initiatives and sustainability efforts to ensuring that the marketing practices themselves are ethical and sustainable. For instance, a brand might launch a campaign that for every product sold, a portion of the proceeds is donated to environmental conservation efforts, directly linking consumer purchases with positive societal outcomes.

Furthermore, social responsibility in marketing extends to the supply chain and production processes. Companies are increasingly transparent about their supply chain practices, showcasing efforts to ensure fair labor practices, reduce carbon footprints, and minimize waste. This transparency not only appeals to consumers' growing demand for ethical products but also sets a precedent in the industry, encouraging others to follow suit.

The rise of digital platforms has provided an effective channel for brands to communicate their social responsibility initiatives. Through social media, companies can engage directly with consumers, sharing stories of their efforts and the impact they have on communities and the environment. These platforms offer an opportunity for authentic engagement, allowing consumers to see the tangible effects of their purchases and the brand's commitment to social responsibility.

However, integrating social responsibility into marketing strategies is not without challenges. Brands must ensure that their efforts are genuine and not merely superficial attempts to appeal to consumer sentiment, often referred to as "greenwashing." Consumers are increasingly savvy and can quickly discern between authentic initiatives and marketing tactics designed to exploit ethical trends without substantial commitment or impact.

Moreover, the integration of social responsibility requires a long-term commitment and a willingness to invest in sustainable practices that may not yield immediate financial returns. It involves a strategic approach that aligns the company's business goals with societal and environmental objectives, creating a balance between profit and purpose.

5.3 MARKETING'S ROLE IN GLOBAL CHALLENGES

Marketing plays a pivotal role in addressing global challenges by influencing consumer behavior, raising awareness, and driving collective action towards sustainable and ethical solutions. In the face of issues such as climate change, social inequality, and public health crises, marketers have the opportunity and responsibility to steer both companies and consumers towards practices that contribute positively to the planet and society.

Influencing Consumer Behavior

One of the most direct ways marketing impacts global challenges is by shaping consumer preferences and encouraging sustainable consumption habits. Through educational campaigns and by promoting eco-friendly and socially responsible products, marketers can help shift demand towards goods that have a lower environmental impact and support fair labor practices. For instance, campaigns that highlight the benefits of reducing single-use plastic consumption have led to a significant increase in the use of reusable products, demonstrating how marketing can contribute to environmental sustainability.

Raising Awareness

Marketing campaigns are powerful tools for raising awareness about global challenges. By leveraging the reach and engagement capabilities of various media platforms, marketers can bring critical issues to the forefront of public consciousness. The partnership between the World Wildlife Fund (WWF) and Snapchat, which created a campaign using augmented reality to highlight the plight of endangered species, serves as a compelling example of how marketing can be used to educate and mobilize action on environmental issues.

Driving Corporate Social Responsibility

Marketing also plays a crucial role in highlighting and promoting a company's corporate social responsibility (CSR) initiatives. By communicating a brand's efforts to address global challenges, such as reducing carbon emissions, supporting community development projects, or advocating for social justice, marketing can enhance a company's reputation and strengthen consumer trust. Patagonia's commitment to environmental conservation and its transparent marketing about the footprint of its products exemplify how companies can use marketing to showcase their contributions to solving global challenges.

Partnering for Impact

Collaborations between businesses, non-profit organizations, and governments can amplify the impact of efforts to address global challenges. Marketing can facilitate these partnerships by identifying synergies, co-creating campaigns, and engaging a wider audience. The collaboration between Unilever and various NGOs on water conservation and hygiene projects demonstrates the potential of partnerships to leverage marketing resources for greater societal benefits.

Ethical Considerations and Authenticity

As marketers engage with global challenges, ethical considerations and authenticity become paramount. Consumers are increasingly skeptical of superficial or exploitative campaigns, often referred to as "greenwashing" or "cause marketing," where companies appear to support a cause without meaningful action or commitment. Authenticity in marketing about a company's role in addressing global challenges is crucial for maintaining credibility and genuinely contributing to positive change.

5.4 CASE STUDIES IN ETHICAL MARKETING

Ethical marketing represents a commitment to honesty, fairness, and responsibility in all advertising and communication practices. It's a powerful approach that not only enhances brand reputation and customer loyalty but also contributes positively to society. Here, we explore several case studies of companies that have successfully implemented ethical marketing strategies, showcasing the potential for businesses to thrive by aligning their operations with ethical principles and social responsibility.

Patagonia: Championing Environmental Sustainability

Patagonia stands as a leading example of ethical marketing through its unwavering commitment to environmental conservation. The company's "Don't Buy This Jacket" campaign, launched to encourage responsible consumption, is a testament to its dedication to sustainability over profits. By urging consumers to consider the environmental impact of their purchases and to buy less, Patagonia reinforced its brand values and attracted a loyal customer base that shares its commitment to the planet. Furthermore, Patagonia's transparent supply chain practices and initiatives, such as the Worn Wear program, which encourages repairing and recycling garments, exemplify its holistic approach to ethical marketing and sustainability.

TOMS Shoes: Pioneering the One-for-One Model

TOMS Shoes introduced the one-for-one business model, promising to donate a pair of shoes to a child in need for every pair purchased. This innovative approach not only addressed a significant social issue — lack of footwear in impoverished communities — but also resonated deeply with consumers, driving sales and brand loyalty. TOMS has since expanded its giving model to include eyewear, clean water, and safe birth services, demonstrating the scalability of ethical marketing strategies that directly contribute to social causes.

Dove: Promoting Real Beauty

Dove's "Real Beauty" campaign is a prime example of ethical marketing in the beauty industry, challenging the conventional standards of beauty and promoting body positivity. By featuring women of various ages, sizes, and ethnicities in its advertisements, Dove sought to widen the definition of beauty and empower women to feel confident in their own skin. This campaign not only elevated Dove's brand image but also sparked important conversations about beauty standards and self-esteem, showcasing the power of marketing to influence societal attitudes and norms.

Ben & Jerry's: Advocating for Social Justice

Ben & Jerry's has long been recognized for its commitment to social justice and environmental issues, incorporating these values into its brand identity and marketing strategies. The company has taken bold stances on matters such as climate change, refugee rights, and racial justice, using its platform to raise awareness and advocate for change. Ben & Jerry's approach to ethical marketing demonstrates how businesses can engage with pressing societal issues in a way that is authentic, impactful, and aligned with their brand values.

Interface: Leading in Sustainable Manufacturing

Interface, a global leader in modular carpeting, embarked on a mission to eliminate its environmental impact by 2020 through its Mission Zero® program. The company's innovative practices include recycling old carpets, reducing greenhouse gas emissions, and pioneering the use of bio-based materials. Interface's transparent communication about its sustainability goals and progress has not only positioned it as an industry leader in environmental responsibility but also attracted customers who prioritize eco-friendly products and practices.

PART II: STRATEGIES AND MANAGEMENT IN MARKETING

Dollar Shave Club's Unique Branding

(AI Generated Photo)

Dollar Shave Club, a startup in the razor market, made a splash with its unique branding and marketing approach. The company's breakthrough came in 2012 with the launch of a low-budget, humorous video featuring CEO Michael Dubin. The video, filled with witty one-liners and a direct sales pitch, introduced the brand's main proposition: high-quality razors delivered to your door at an affordable price.

The unconventional approach distinguished Dollar Shave Club from its competitors, who traditionally relied on more sophisticated and serious advertising. The video went viral, gaining millions of views and catapulting the brand into the spotlight. This marketing success highlighted the effectiveness of understanding and targeting the right audience with a message that resonates with them. Dollar Shave Club's approach proved that humor and directness could be powerful tools in cutting through a crowded market.

CHAPTER 6. BLUEPRINTS FOR MARKETING STRATEGY AND PLANNING

The discipline of marketing, with its rich tapestry of history, strategy, and consumer-centric evolution, serves as the backbone for crafting the blueprints of marketing strategy and planning. This chapter distills the essence of marketing into actionable strategies and plans that not only drive business success but also foster a meaningful impact on society. Drawing upon the foundational insights from the introductory exploration of marketing, we delve into the strategic and planning phases that encapsulate the dynamic interplay between creativity, strategy, and a deep understanding of consumer behavior.

Marketing, at its core, is about creating narratives that resonate, building enduring relationships, and making a significant societal impact. This journey from a production-focused approach to a customer-centric paradigm underscores the transformation of marketing strategies to meet and exceed the evolving desires of consumers. Reflecting on the historical milestones and theoretical frameworks that have shaped marketing, this chapter aims to guide readers through the intricacies of developing comprehensive marketing strategies and plans that align with modern business imperatives and societal values.

In the evolving landscape of digital marketing, where traditional advertising methods were becoming increasingly ineffective, HubSpot emerged as a trailblazer with its innovative inbound marketing strategy. This case study, integral to understanding the impact of crafting a comprehensive marketing plan, illustrates HubSpot's journey to redefine engagement through content marketing.

The Inception of Inbound Marketing

HubSpot, founded in 2006 by Brian Halligan and Dharmesh Shah, recognized early on the shifting paradigms of consumer behavior. They observed that people were tuning out traditional, interruption-based marketing techniques and gravitating towards online content that was helpful, informative, and entertaining. Seizing upon this insight, HubSpot coined the term "inbound marketing," a strategy focused on attracting customers through relevant and helpful content.

Building a Content Marketing Empire

Central to HubSpot's inbound marketing strategy was its commitment to creating high-quality, relevant content tailored to the interests and challenges of its target audience. HubSpot meticulously crafted a variety of content forms—blog posts, industry reports, webinars, and more—to educate and engage potential customers at different stages of the buyer's journey.

The blog, in particular, became the cornerstone of HubSpot's content marketing plan. It was designed not just as a platform for sharing insights but as a tool for solving real-world problems faced by marketers and business owners. Through consistent, value-driven content, HubSpot established itself as a thought leader in the digital marketing space.

Driving Growth Through Engagement

HubSpot's content marketing efforts paid off spectacularly, with its blog attracting millions of visitors each year. This unprecedented level of engagement was no accident; it was the result of a well-executed plan that leveraged SEO best practices, social media marketing, and email marketing to distribute and amplify its content.

By focusing on the needs and interests of its audience, HubSpot was able to drive significant traffic to its website. More importantly, this strategy helped convert visitors into leads and, ultimately, customers. The educational nature of the content fostered trust and credibility, positioning HubSpot not just as a service provider but as a valuable resource for the marketing community.

Lessons Learned

HubSpot's success story serves as a powerful example for businesses looking to navigate the complexities of digital marketing. It underscores the importance of understanding consumer behavior, the potential of content marketing in building brand authority, and the need for a cohesive, well-planned marketing strategy that aligns with audience needs.

The case of HubSpot highlights several key lessons:

Content Is King: Delivering consistent, high-quality content tailored to your audience can establish your brand as an industry leader.

Engagement Drives Growth: By engaging with your audience through relevant content, you can drive traffic, generate leads, and grow your business.

Adaptability is Essential: The digital marketing landscape is ever-evolving. Businesses must remain agile, ready to adapt their strategies to meet changing consumer behaviors and market dynamics.

6.1 CRAFTING A COMPREHENSIVE MARKETING PLAN

In the intricate dance of business strategy, a comprehensive marketing plan acts not merely as a guide but as a compass, directing companies through the competitive landscapes they navigate. This chapter embarks on a deep dive into the art and science of crafting a marketing plan that not only resonates with the company's vision but is also adaptable, measurable, and capable of driving sustainable growth.

The Essence of a Marketing Plan

A marketing plan is a strategic blueprint that outlines a company's advertising and marketing efforts for the coming year. It is a document that details how a business will reach its target market, articulating the strategies and tactics that will be employed to drive sales and enhance brand recognition. The plan encompasses a wide array of elements, including market research, marketing objectives, target markets, marketing strategies, budgets, and performance metrics.

Initiating with Market Research

The foundation of a compelling marketing plan is robust market research. This initial step involves gathering and analyzing information about the market, including customer demographics, preferences, needs, buying behavior, and a detailed analysis of competitors. Market research provides the insights necessary to make informed decisions and tailor marketing strategies that align with the target audience's expectations and the competitive dynamics of the market.

Defining Marketing Objectives

Clear, concise, and measurable marketing objectives are critical to the plan's success. These objectives should be aligned with the business's overall goals and capable of guiding the direction of marketing efforts. Employing the SMART criteria ensures that objectives are Specific, Measurable, Achievable, Relevant, and Time-bound. Whether the aim is to increase brand awareness, boost sales, enhance customer engagement, or enter new markets, each objective must have corresponding metrics to evaluate success.

Strategizing for Success

With objectives in place, the next step is to formulate the marketing strategy. This involves selecting the target market segments to pursue and determining the positioning that the product or service will take in the market. Strategies may encompass a broad range of activities, from product development and pricing strategies to distribution channels and promotional tactics. The strategy section should provide a clear roadmap of how the objectives will be achieved, taking into account the strengths, weaknesses, opportunities, and threats identified in the situational analysis.

Tactics and Action Plans

Translating strategy into action, this section delineates the specific tactics and activities that will be employed to implement the strategy. It outlines the marketing mix—product, price, place, promotion—and details how each element will be leveraged to reach the marketing objectives. Action plans are comprehensive, including timelines, responsible parties, and required resources, ensuring that each aspect of the marketing strategy is actionable and measurable.

Budgeting for Impact

An effective marketing plan includes a detailed budget that allocates resources across various marketing activities. The budget should reflect the priorities of the marketing plan, ensuring that resources are invested in areas that will deliver the greatest impact. Approaches to budgeting, such as the percentage-of-sales method or the objective-and-task method, offer frameworks for allocating funds in a manner that supports the strategic goals of the marketing plan.

Evaluating and Adjusting

The final cornerstone of a marketing plan is the framework for evaluation and adjustment. This involves setting up key performance indicators (KPIs) and regular review periods to assess the effectiveness of marketing activities against the set objectives. Performance evaluation enables marketers to identify areas of success and areas needing improvement, facilitating agile adjustments to strategies and tactics in response to market feedback and changing conditions.

6.2 ESSENTIALS OF THE STRATEGIC MARKETING PROCESS

In the dynamic theatre of business, strategic marketing plays the starring role, orchestrating the myriad decisions and actions that propel a company towards its goals. The strategic marketing process is a framework that allows businesses to align their marketing initiatives with their broader objectives, ensuring coherent and effective market engagement. This chapter delves into the critical components of the strategic marketing process, guiding readers through the essential steps necessary to craft strategies that are not only visionary but also actionable and aligned with the ever-changing market landscape.

Understanding the Strategic Marketing Process

The strategic marketing process is a deliberate and structured approach to developing and implementing marketing strategies. It involves a series of steps that guide businesses from initial analysis through strategy development, implementation, and ongoing evaluation. This cyclical process ensures that marketing efforts are continuously aligned with business goals, market needs, and environmental changes.

Step 1: Situation Analysis

At the heart of the strategic marketing process lies the situation analysis, a comprehensive examination of a company's current market position and the external and internal factors that influence its marketing strategies. This analysis typically includes a SWOT (Strengths, Weaknesses, Opportunities, Threats) analysis, market research, and competitive intelligence. The goal is to develop a nuanced understanding of the market dynamics, customer needs, and the company's capabilities, laying the groundwork for informed strategic planning.

Step 2: Setting Marketing Objectives

Clear, measurable marketing objectives set the direction for the strategic marketing process. These objectives should be directly aligned with the company's overall goals and designed to be SMART: Specific, Measurable,

Achievable, Relevant, and Time-bound. Objectives can range from increasing market share and improving brand awareness to enhancing customer loyalty and launching new products or services.

Step 3: Strategic Development
With a firm understanding of the market and clear objectives in place, the next step is to develop the marketing strategy. This involves deciding on the target market segments, positioning the product or service in the marketplace, and determining the competitive advantage. The strategy articulates how the company will create value for customers and differentiate itself from competitors, serving as a blueprint for tactical planning and execution.

Step 4: Tactical Planning
Tactical planning translates the marketing strategy into specific actions and initiatives. This stage involves detailing the marketing mix—the 4Ps (Product, Price, Place, Promotion)—and other tactical elements that will be used to achieve the marketing objectives. It includes decisions on product development, pricing strategies, distribution channels, promotional campaigns, and sales initiatives. Each tactic is assigned resources, timelines, and responsibilities to ensure effective implementation.

Step 5: Implementation
The implementation phase is where plans are put into action. It requires careful coordination of resources, effective communication within the organization, and meticulous management of the marketing activities. Successful implementation hinges on the ability to adapt to challenges and opportunities that arise during execution, requiring flexibility and responsiveness from the marketing team.

Step 6: Evaluation and Control
The final step in the strategic marketing process is evaluation and control, where the outcomes of marketing activities are measured against the set objectives. This involves analyzing performance data, assessing ROI, and monitoring market feedback. The insights gained from this evaluation are crucial for identifying areas of success and areas needing improvement, informing adjustments to strategies and tactics.

6.3 AGILE MARKETING STRATEGIES

In today's fast-paced and ever-evolving market landscape, agility has become a cornerstone of effective marketing. Agile marketing strategies represent a paradigm shift from traditional, plan-based marketing approaches to more flexible, iterative methods that allow businesses to respond quickly to changes in the market, consumer behavior, or technology. This chapter explores the principles of agile marketing and how they can be applied to develop strategies that are not only responsive but also focused on delivering value to the customer and the business.

The Agile Marketing Framework

Agile marketing is inspired by the principles of agile software development, emphasizing speed, flexibility, and collaboration. It involves breaking down large marketing initiatives into smaller, manageable tasks (often called "sprints") that are completed in short cycles. This framework allows marketing teams to test ideas, gather feedback, and iterate on their strategies in real-time, making adjustments based on actual performance and changing conditions.

Key Principles of Agile Marketing

Customer-Centric Focus: Agile marketing prioritizes the customer's needs and experiences above all else, ensuring that marketing efforts are always aligned with delivering value to the target audience.

Adaptive Planning: While traditional marketing plans are often set in stone, agile marketing advocates for adaptive planning that can change as needed, allowing for responsiveness to market dynamics.

Rapid Execution: The emphasis is on executing tasks quickly and efficiently, reducing the time from planning to action, and allowing for immediate feedback and adjustment.

Iterative Approach: Agile marketing is characterized by a cycle of planning, executing, learning, and iterating, allowing strategies to evolve based on insights gained from real-world interactions.

Collaborative Teams: Cross-functional teams work collaboratively in agile marketing, breaking down silos to enhance communication and leveraging diverse skills for innovative solutions.

Implementing Agile Marketing Strategies

Define Clear Objectives: Even in agile marketing, clear, measurable objectives are crucial. These should align with broader business goals but be flexible enough to adapt to new insights and market changes.

Build Cross-Functional Teams: Agile marketing requires teams that bring together diverse expertise, including creative, analytical, digital, and strategic skills. These teams work collaboratively in sprints to achieve specific objectives.

Develop a Backlog of Marketing Initiatives: Create a prioritized list of marketing tasks and projects, known as a backlog. This backlog is continuously updated based on shifting priorities, new opportunities, or feedback from completed tasks.

Work in Sprints: Break down work into short, manageable periods (sprints), typically ranging from two to four weeks. Each sprint focuses on completing a set of tasks from the backlog, allowing for rapid testing and iteration.

Hold Regular Stand-ups and Reviews: Daily stand-up meetings keep team members aligned and focused, while sprint reviews assess what was accomplished and what can be improved. This continuous feedback loop is essential for agile marketing.

Measure and Adjust: Use data-driven insights to measure the impact of marketing activities. Key performance indicators (KPIs) should be reviewed regularly to inform adjustments to tactics and strategy.

Benefits and Challenges

Agile marketing offers several benefits, including increased speed to market, improved responsiveness to customer needs, enhanced team collaboration, and a greater ability to adjust to market volatility. However, it also poses challenges, such as the need for cultural change within organizations, the requirement for constant communication, and the potential for burnout due to the fast-paced nature of agile cycles.

6.4 CROSS-FUNCTIONAL TEAM INTEGRATION IN MARKETING

In the modern business ecosystem, where innovation and speed are paramount, the integration of cross-functional teams in marketing has emerged as a strategic imperative. This approach breaks down the traditional silos between departments, fostering a culture of collaboration and shared purpose that drives marketing effectiveness and organizational agility. This chapter delves into the concept of cross-functional team integration in marketing, outlining its benefits, challenges, and strategies for successful implementation.

The Concept of Cross-Functional Teams

Cross-functional teams consist of members with diverse expertise and backgrounds from different departments within an organization, such as marketing, sales, product development, customer service, and IT. These teams are formed to work on specific projects or initiatives, leveraging their varied skills to achieve common goals. In the context of marketing, cross-functional teams collaborate on campaigns, product launches, customer experience strategies, and more, ensuring a holistic and aligned approach to market engagement.

Benefits of Cross-Functional Team Integration

Enhanced Creativity and Innovation: Bringing together diverse perspectives and skills fosters creativity, leading to more innovative marketing solutions and strategies.

Improved Agility: Cross-functional teams can respond more swiftly to market changes, customer feedback, and emerging trends, enhancing the organization's overall agility.

Increased Efficiency: Collaboration across departments reduces duplication of efforts, streamlines processes, and accelerates the execution of marketing initiatives.

Better Decision-Making: The integration of insights from various functional areas leads to more informed decision-making, ensuring that marketing strategies are grounded in a comprehensive understanding of the business and its customers.

Enhanced Customer Experience: A collaborative approach ensures that all touchpoints along the customer journey are considered, leading to a more cohesive and satisfying customer experience.

Challenges and Solutions

While the integration of cross-functional teams offers numerous benefits, it also presents challenges that need to be navigated carefully:

Communication Barriers: Differences in language, priorities, and working styles among departments can hinder effective communication. Regular team meetings, clear communication protocols, and the use of collaborative tools can help overcome these barriers.

Alignment of Goals: Aligning the objectives of diverse team members can be challenging. Setting clear, shared goals at the outset of a project and ensuring they are aligned with overall business objectives can mitigate this issue.

Resource Allocation: Competing priorities for resources and time can create friction. Transparent and fair resource allocation processes, along with executive support, are crucial for addressing this challenge.

Cultural Differences: Organizational silos can breed a culture of isolation rather than collaboration. Building a culture that values diversity, openness, and teamwork is essential for the success of cross-functional teams.

Strategies for Successful Integration

Leadership Support: Strong endorsement from leadership is essential to foster a culture that values and supports cross-functional collaboration.

Clear Roles and Responsibilities: Defining clear roles, responsibilities, and accountability for team members helps in managing expectations and enhancing collaboration.

Effective Project Management: Employing project management best practices and tools ensures that cross-functional initiatives are executed efficiently and effectively.

Continuous Learning and Improvement: Regularly reviewing the performance of cross-functional teams, celebrating successes, and learning from challenges are key to continuous improvement.

In the realm of marketing, few brands have managed to carve out a niche as distinct and powerful as Red Bull. This energy drink giant has transcended its product category to become a symbol of extreme sports, adventure, and high energy lifestyle. The case of Red Bull offers invaluable insights into the crafting of a comprehensive marketing plan that leverages unique brand positioning and targeted marketing efforts.

Crafting a Comprehensive Marketing Plan

Red Bull's marketing strategy is a testament to the power of aligning a brand with a lifestyle and set of values that resonate deeply with its target audience. Through meticulous market research, both internal and external, including website analytics, customer surveys, and focus groups, Red Bull has continually updated its buyer profile to ensure its marketing strategies remain relevant and effective (Starting Business).

A cornerstone of Red Bull's approach is its eclectic marketing delivery, which spans both online and offline channels. Influencer digital marketing plays a significant role, with the brand collaborating with elite athletes and extreme sports personalities. This not only broadens Red Bull's reach but also reinforces brand affinity among new and existing audiences. User-generated content and international competitions like the Red Bull Illume further promote a sense of community and engagement, turning a simple marketing tactic into a powerful campaign (Starting Business).

Event Sponsorship and Media Presence

Red Bull's sponsorship of sporting events and ownership of sports teams, such as the Red Bull F1 and NASCAR teams, along with football and ice hockey teams, underlines the brand's commitment to its high-energy theme. This strategy not only differentiates Red Bull from its competitors but also builds a loyal community among its consumers (Starting Business).

Additionally, Red Bull's investment in TV streaming and advertising, including the ownership of a video streaming platform and significant investment in TV commercials, ensures that the excitement around its brand

and sponsored events reaches a global audience. Red Bull's print promotions and the distribution of its print magazine further extend its reach, capturing each segment of its target consumer group (Starting Business).

Innovative Distribution and Sales Channels

Red Bull's distribution strategy, focusing on exclusivity and unconventional retail channels like gas stations, convenience stores, and vending machines, has helped establish its presence in both traditional and overlooked markets. The brand's innovative approach to distribution in emerging markets through a network of independent distributors has enabled Red Bull to gain a foothold where other brands might struggle (Cascade Strategy).

Product Innovation and Branding

Red Bull's focus on product functionality and flavor innovation, along with distinctive packaging and branding, has kept the brand at the forefront of trends in the beverage industry. The iconic Red Bull can design, along with new flavors and packaging formats, has contributed significantly to the brand's strong identity and market leadership (Beloved Brands).

The Power of Storytelling and Social Media

Red Bull's marketing strategy shines in its ability to tell a compelling story that appeals to its audience, from extreme sports to music festivals. By positioning its product as providing the energy and courage to attempt daring feats, Red Bull has created content that feels alive and in motion, mirroring the brand's high-energy aesthetic. This dynamic presence on social media and strategic sponsorships expose the Red Bull brand to new audiences and maintain its relevance among its target market (Mix With Marketing).

Red Bull's journey from a humble beginning to a mega-brand is a remarkable case study in marketing, illustrating the effectiveness of a well-crafted marketing plan that places audience interests at the forefront. By focusing on storytelling, consistent branding, and creating a solid foundation of content that resonates with its target market, Red Bull has established a unique position in the market that goes beyond selling an energy drink to promoting a lifestyle.

CHAPTER 7. SEGMENTATION, TARGETING, AND POSITIONING (STP)

In the dynamic landscape of marketing, the strategic trifecta of Segmentation, Targeting, and Positioning (STP) stands as a cornerstone, shaping the way businesses identify and connect with their core audiences. This chapter delves into the essence of STP, exploring how it empowers marketers to carve out a distinctive space in a crowded marketplace, tailor strategies to meet specific customer needs, and ultimately drive competitive advantage and customer loyalty.

Starting with Segmentation, the chapter unveils the diversity within markets and the process of identifying niches with specific needs, behaviors, or interests through various criteria including demographic, psychographic, geographic, and behavioral factors. It then transitions to Targeting, highlighting the importance of evaluating each segment's attractiveness and deciding which segment(s) to serve. This step is pivotal in determining where a company should concentrate its efforts and resources for maximum impact, requiring a deep analysis of segment size, growth potential, competitive presence, and alignment with the company's objectives and capabilities.

The culmination of the STP process, Positioning, shifts the focus to creating a distinct image or identity for the product or service in the mind of the target market. It involves differentiating from competitors and clarifying why a brand is the best choice for the identified target segments. Effective positioning is achieved through the strategic development of key messages that highlight the unique benefits and features of the product or service, tailored to the needs and preferences of the target audience.

The chapter further discusses implementing STP for competitive advantage, addressing the model's strategic framework that guides all aspects of marketing strategy and execution, influencing product development, pricing, distribution, and promotional strategies. It emphasizes how segmentation informs product development, targeting directs resource allocation, and positioning shapes the communication strategy. Additionally, it explores challenges and considerations in maintaining the relevance and effectiveness of the STP strategy in an increasingly connected and digital world.

By providing a comprehensive overview of the STP process, this chapter equips readers with the knowledge and tools to navigate the complexities of market segmentation, target selection, and brand positioning, laying the groundwork for developing marketing strategies that not only meet the immediate needs of the business but also anticipate future market developments and consumer trends.

7.1 MASTERING MARKET SEGMENTATION TECHNIQUES

Market segmentation is the first and arguably most critical step in the STP (Segmentation, Targeting, and Positioning) process. It involves dividing a broad market into smaller, distinct groups of consumers with common needs, behaviors, or characteristics who might require separate products or marketing mixes. Mastering market segmentation techniques enables marketers to tailor their strategies precisely, enhancing efficiency, and improving customer satisfaction. This section explores the various segmentation techniques, offering insights into their application and benefits.

Types of Market Segmentation

Demographic Segmentation: This is one of the most straightforward and widely used forms of segmentation, dividing the market based on variables such as age, gender, income, education level, and family size. Demographic segmentation helps marketers to target specific products to the right audience, making it easier to meet the particular needs of different consumer groups.

Geographic Segmentation: Geographic segmentation divides the market based on location, such as countries, cities, neighborhoods, or postal codes. It considers geographical factors that might affect consumer needs and preferences, allowing for strategies that cater to local tastes, cultural differences, or climatic conditions.

Psychographic Segmentation: This technique delves deeper into the psychological aspects of consumer behavior, segmenting the market based on lifestyle, values, attitudes, and interests. Psychographic segmentation provides a richer understanding of consumers, enabling brands to connect on a more personal and emotional level.

Behavioral Segmentation: Behavioral segmentation divides consumers based on their knowledge of, attitude towards, use of, or response to a product. It includes criteria such as purchase occasions, benefits sought, user status, and loyalty status. This segmentation is crucial for tailoring marketing messages based on consumer behavior patterns, enhancing engagement and conversion rates.

Implementing Effective Segmentation

Successful market segmentation requires a deep understanding of the market and the target consumers. The process involves several key steps:

Identifying Segmentation Variables: Start by determining which segmentation criteria are most relevant to your product or service. This could involve a combination of demographic, geographic, psychographic, and behavioral factors.

Research and Analysis: Conduct market research to gather data on potential customers and analyze this information to identify distinct segments within the broader market.

Segment Evaluation: Assess the identified segments for viability. Consider factors such as segment size, growth potential, accessibility, and compatibility with the company's objectives and resources.

Select Target Segments: Based on the evaluation, select the most attractive and viable segments to target. This decision should align with the company's overall strategic goals and market position.

Develop Profiles: Create detailed profiles for each target segment, outlining their specific needs, preferences, behaviors, and demographics. These profiles serve as the foundation for crafting tailored marketing strategies.

Challenges and Considerations

While market segmentation offers numerous benefits, it also presents challenges. Marketers must ensure that segments are measurable, accessible, substantial, and actionable. Over-segmentation can lead to unnecessarily complicated marketing strategies, while under-segmentation might result in missed opportunities for differentiation. Moreover, the dynamic nature of markets demands continuous monitoring and adjustment of segmentation strategies to reflect changing consumer behaviors and market conditions.

7.2 CRAFTING EFFECTIVE TARGETING STRATEGIES

After segmenting the market into distinct groups, the next critical step in the STP process is targeting. Crafting effective targeting strategies involves selecting the most attractive segment(s) to serve, a decision that profoundly influences the marketing mix and overall strategic direction. This section explores the principles and methodologies for developing targeted marketing strategies that align with business objectives and market opportunities.

Understanding Targeting Strategies

Targeting can be approached through several strategies, each suited to different market conditions and organizational goals:

Undifferentiated (Mass) Targeting: This strategy treats the market as a whole, focusing on what is common in the needs of consumers rather than on what is different. It is effective in markets where the product's appeal is universal, but it risks overlooking the nuanced preferences of different consumer groups.

Differentiated (Segmented) Targeting: Companies adopting this strategy target several market segments with distinct offerings for each. It allows for more tailored marketing efforts but requires more resources to implement effectively.

Concentrated (Niche) Targeting: Concentrated targeting focuses on a single market segment, allowing a company to direct its resources to becoming an expert in that niche. This strategy is particularly beneficial for smaller companies with limited resources.

Micro (Local or One-to-One) Targeting: This approach goes even further by focusing on individual customers or very small segments. It is often used in conjunction with personalized marketing and is facilitated by digital technologies that track consumer behaviors and preferences.

Criteria for Selecting Target Markets

Effective targeting requires a careful evaluation of each segment's attractiveness. Marketers typically consider several criteria in this process:

Segment Size and Growth: Assess the current size and anticipated growth of the segment to ensure it can support the company's objectives.

Competitive Landscape: Understand the level of competition within the segment. A less crowded segment might offer more opportunities for differentiation.

Compatibility with Organizational Goals and Resources: The chosen segment should align with the company's strategic goals and be reachable given its resources and capabilities.

Profitability Potential: Evaluate the segment's profitability, considering factors such as the cost to serve, potential pricing strategies, and customer lifetime value.

Developing Targeting Strategies

Once the target segments are identified, developing an effective strategy involves:

Aligning Product Offerings with Segment Needs: Tailor your product or service offerings to meet the specific needs and preferences of the target segment. This might involve customization or differentiation of products.

Optimizing the Marketing Mix: Adjust the marketing mix (product, price, place, promotion) to appeal directly to the targeted segment. This includes developing targeted promotional campaigns, selecting appropriate distribution channels, and setting prices that reflect the segment's value perception.

Leveraging Technology for Precision Targeting: Use digital technologies, data analytics, and CRM systems to gain deeper insights into the target segment and enable more precise and personalized marketing efforts.

Measuring and Adjusting Strategies: Continuously monitor the effectiveness of targeting strategies through key performance indicators (KPIs). Be prepared to adjust tactics in response to market feedback and changing conditions.

Challenges in Targeting

Crafting effective targeting strategies is not without challenges. Marketers must navigate the complexities of changing consumer behaviors, data privacy concerns, and the need for balance between personalization and intrusion. Moreover, the dynamic nature of markets requires ongoing vigilance and adaptability to ensure that targeting strategies remain relevant and effective.

7.3 UNRAVELING THE INTRICACIES OF POSITIONING

Positioning, the final cornerstone in the Segmentation, Targeting, and Positioning (STP) framework, is pivotal in defining how a brand or product is perceived in the minds of the target audience relative to competitors. This strategic process involves crafting a distinct identity and value proposition that resonates with the targeted segments, setting the foundation for all marketing communications and strategies. This chapter delves into the intricacies of effective positioning, exploring techniques to establish a compelling market presence that captivates and retains consumer interest.

The Essence of Positioning

Positioning is not merely about how a company sees its product but more importantly, about shaping consumer perceptions. It's the art of aligning a product's features, benefits, and value with the specific needs, preferences, and expectations of the target segment. Effective positioning differentiates a brand in a crowded market, highlighting its unique attributes and reasons why it is the superior choice.

Steps in Developing a Positioning Strategy

Identifying Competitive Advantages: Begin by assessing the strengths of the product or service, focusing on features or benefits that are unique and valuable to the target audience. This could include superior quality, innovative features, exceptional service, or cost-effectiveness.

Understanding the Competitive Landscape: Analyze competitors to identify gaps in the market or areas where your product can offer superior value. Understanding competitor positioning is crucial to carve out a unique space in the market.

Defining the Positioning Statement: A positioning statement succinctly articulates the brand's unique value proposition and the target segment it serves. It serves as a guiding star for marketing strategies, ensuring consistency in messaging across all touchpoints.

Communicating the Positioning: Implement the positioning through targeted marketing campaigns, packaging, product design, and customer experience strategies. Every consumer interaction should reinforce the brand's positioning.

Positioning Techniques

Several techniques can be employed to establish a strong position in the market:

Benefit Positioning: Focus on a unique benefit that the product offers, which is not available from competitors.

Problem-Solution Positioning: Highlight a particular problem faced by the target market and position the product as the best solution.

Price-Quality Positioning: Position the product as offering the best value, whether it's the highest quality at a premium price or solid quality at a low price.

Lifestyle Positioning: Associate the product with a particular lifestyle or attitude, appealing to consumers' aspirations or self-image.

Category Positioning: Position the product as the leader in a certain category or create a new category where the product is the pioneer.

Challenges in Positioning

Positioning in a dynamic market environment presents several challenges:

Maintaining Relevance: Consumer preferences and competitive landscapes are constantly evolving, requiring brands to adapt their positioning to stay relevant.

Overcoming Market Saturation: In highly competitive markets, finding a unique positioning can be challenging, necessitating creative and innovative approaches.

Consistency Across Channels: Ensuring that the positioning is consistently communicated across all marketing channels and touchpoints can be complex, especially in a multi-channel marketing environment.

Measuring the Effectiveness of Positioning

The impact of positioning strategies should be continuously monitored and measured. This can be achieved through brand perception surveys, market share analysis, customer feedback, and monitoring of marketing campaign performance. Adjustments should be made based on these insights to refine and strengthen the positioning over time.

7.4 MICRO-SEGMENTATION AND PERSONALIZATION

In the current era of marketing, where competition is intense and consumers demand more tailored experiences, micro-segmentation and personalization have emerged as critical strategies for achieving a competitive edge. These approaches refine traditional segmentation methods, breaking down larger market segments into smaller, more precise groups to deliver highly customized marketing messages and product offerings. This chapter explores the concepts of micro-segmentation and personalization, illustrating their importance in enhancing customer engagement, satisfaction, and loyalty.

Micro-Segmentation: The Finer Slice

Micro-segmentation involves dividing the market into even smaller segments based on very specific criteria, such as lifestyle choices, purchasing behaviors, or interaction patterns with the brand. Unlike broader segmentation, which might categorize consumers into large groups based on common characteristics, micro-segmentation drills down to the nuances of individual preferences and behaviors, creating segments that may be as small as a niche group or even individual consumers.

Key Benefits of Micro-Segmentation

Enhanced Targeting Accuracy: By understanding the distinct characteristics of smaller segments, marketers can tailor their strategies with greater precision, significantly improving the effectiveness of their campaigns.

Increased Customer Engagement: Tailored messages resonate more deeply with consumers, leading to higher engagement rates.

Improved Conversion Rates: Personalized offerings that closely match the specific needs and desires of a micro-segment are more likely to convert interest into purchases.

Efficient Resource Allocation: Focusing resources on highly targeted segments reduces waste and enhances ROI.

Personalization: The Ultimate Goal

Personalization is the natural progression from micro-segmentation, where marketing strategies are tailored to the individual level, offering unique experiences based on a consumer's specific preferences, behaviors, and history with the brand. This can range from personalized emails and product recommendations to customized website experiences and targeted advertising.

Implementing Personalization Strategies

Data Collection and Analysis: The foundation of personalization is data. Collecting detailed data from various touchpoints and analyzing it to understand individual consumer behaviors and preferences is crucial.

Technology Utilization: Leveraging advanced technologies such as AI and machine learning can help in processing large datasets to identify patterns, predict behaviors, and automate personalized interactions.

Content Customization: Develop a variety of content that can be dynamically adjusted and served to individuals based on their identified preferences and behaviors.

Continuous Optimization: Personalization is an ongoing process. Continuous testing, measurement, and refinement are necessary to adapt to changing consumer preferences and improve the effectiveness of personalized strategies.

Challenges in Micro-Segmentation and Personalization

While the benefits are clear, these strategies also present challenges:

Data Privacy and Security: Collecting and utilizing consumer data raises concerns about privacy and security. Brands must navigate these issues carefully, ensuring compliance with regulations and maintaining consumer trust.

Complexity and Resource Requirements: Implementing sophisticated micro-segmentation and personalization strategies requires significant resources, including advanced technology platforms and skilled personnel.

Maintaining Authenticity: There is a fine line between personalization and intrusion. Brands must strive to maintain authenticity and respect consumer boundaries to avoid negative perceptions.

7.5 AI-DRIVEN POSITIONING STRATEGIES

The integration of artificial intelligence (AI) into marketing strategies marks a revolutionary shift in how businesses position their brands, products, and services in the marketplace. AI-driven positioning strategies leverage the power of advanced analytics, machine learning, and data processing capabilities to uncover deep insights into consumer behavior, preferences, and trends. This chapter explores how AI is transforming the landscape of positioning strategies, enabling more dynamic, responsive, and personalized approaches to capturing consumer attention and loyalty.

The Role of AI in Positioning

AI technologies offer unprecedented capabilities in analyzing vast amounts of data to identify patterns, predict consumer behaviors, and generate insights that were previously inaccessible. In the context of positioning, AI can be used to:

Analyze Market Trends: AI algorithms can sift through global market data to identify emerging trends, providing businesses with early indicators of shifts in consumer preferences and competitive dynamics.

Understand Consumer Behavior: By analyzing data from social media, online interactions, and purchase histories, AI can offer detailed insights into individual consumer behaviors and preferences, enabling more precise targeting and positioning strategies.

Optimize Messaging and Content: AI tools can test and refine marketing messages, visual content, and calls to action in real-time, determining what resonates best with target audiences to strengthen positioning efforts.

Personalize Consumer Experiences: Leveraging AI, businesses can create highly personalized consumer experiences that align with their positioning strategy, tailoring product recommendations, content, and marketing messages to individual consumer profiles.

Implementing AI-Driven Positioning Strategies

Implementing AI-driven positioning strategies involves several key steps:

Data Collection and Integration: Collect comprehensive data from various touchpoints, including online interactions, customer feedback, and market research. Integrate this data into a unified platform for analysis.

AI Model Development: Develop machine learning models tailored to analyze the collected data, capable of identifying trends, predicting behaviors, and generating insights relevant to positioning strategies.

Insight Application: Apply the insights derived from AI analysis to inform positioning decisions. This could involve identifying niche markets, tailoring product features, or customizing marketing messages.

Continuous Learning and Adjustment: AI models should be designed for continuous learning, allowing them to evolve with new data. This enables positioning strategies to remain dynamic and responsive to market changes.

Challenges and Considerations

While AI-driven positioning offers significant advantages, it also presents challenges:

Data Privacy and Ethics: The use of consumer data for AI analysis must be handled with strict adherence to privacy laws and ethical standards, ensuring consumer trust is maintained.

Complexity and Resource Requirements: Developing and implementing AI-driven positioning strategies requires significant investment in technology and expertise, which may be challenging for smaller organizations.

Avoiding Over-Reliance on AI: While AI can provide valuable insights, human judgment remains crucial in interpreting data and making strategic decisions. Balancing AI analysis with human creativity and intuition is essential.

CHAPTER 8. MANAGING PRODUCTS AND BRANDS

In the intricate dance of modern business, the strategic management of products and brands emerges as a pivotal performance. It's a discipline that not only requires an understanding of market dynamics but also an ability to forge a deep connection with consumers. This chapter delves into the essence of managing products and brands, illustrating how businesses can nurture their portfolios to foster growth, cultivate brand equity, and sustain competitive advantage.

The symphony of product management plays a crucial role, acting as the conductor in the orchestra of business strategy. It harmonizes the elements of development, launch, lifecycle, and evolution, ensuring that each product performs its part flawlessly, contributing to the overall success of the brand. From the innovation and development stage, where new ideas are nurtured and transformed into tangible offerings, to strategic launch and lifecycle management, this section outlines the vital steps in guiding products through their market journey.

Furthermore, brand management is explored as a strategic effort to build and sustain a brand's identity, reputation, and equity in the consumer's psyche. Establishing a strong brand identity and clear positioning is foundational, serving as a beacon guiding all branding efforts and ensuring consistency across touchpoints. The strength of a brand, measured by its equity, translates into consumer loyalty, allowing brands to command premium pricing and foster sustainable growth. This chapter also highlights the importance of managing a brand portfolio and engaging with consumers across multiple platforms in the digital age, enhancing the collective strength of the brand family.

Lastly, navigating the product life cycle (PLC) is discussed, offering strategies for effective management across its distinct phases: Introduction,

Growth, Maturity, and Decline. Understanding and navigating the PLC is crucial for marketers and product managers to maximize a product's impact and longevity in the market

8.1 NAVIGATING THE PRODUCT LIFE CYCLE

The journey of a product from its inception to retirement is marked by various stages, each presenting unique challenges and opportunities. Understanding and navigating the product life cycle (PLC) is crucial for marketers and product managers to maximize a product's impact and longevity in the market. This sub-chapter explores the intricacies of the PLC, offering strategies for effective management across its distinct phases: Introduction, Growth, Maturity, and Decline.

Introduction Stage

The introduction stage marks a product's debut in the market. It's characterized by low sales, high costs per customer acquisition, and limited competition. The primary focus during this stage is to build awareness and stimulate demand.

Strategies for the Introduction Stage:

Invest in targeted marketing campaigns to build product awareness.

Employ promotional strategies to encourage trial and adoption.

Focus on education and information to highlight the product's value proposition.

Growth Stage

As the product gains acceptance, it enters the growth stage, characterized by rapidly increasing sales, improving profitability, and escalating competition. The goal during this phase is to solidify market position and brand preference.

Strategies for the Growth Stage:

Enhance product features and quality to differentiate from competitors.

Expand distribution channels to increase market accessibility.

Intensify marketing efforts focusing on brand loyalty to retain early adopters.

Maturity Stage

The maturity stage represents the peak of a product's life cycle, where sales growth starts to slow down due to market saturation. Profitability remains high, but the competitive landscape becomes more intense.

Strategies for the Maturity Stage:

Diversify product offerings through variations or improvements to rejuvenate consumer interest.

Optimize pricing strategies to balance competitiveness and profitability.

Invest in customer relationship management to enhance loyalty and encourage repeat purchases.

Decline Stage

Eventually, every product faces a decline in sales and profitability, often due to technological advancements, shifts in consumer preferences, or increased competition. Decisions during this stage involve managing the decline profitably or deciding to discontinue the product.

Strategies for the Decline Stage:

Reduce costs and reallocate resources to more profitable items.

Consider product discontinuation or sell-off strategies if recovery is unfeasible.

Explore opportunities for product repurposing or targeting new markets.

Cross-Stage Considerations

Successfully navigating the PLC requires not only stage-specific strategies but also a cross-stage approach that includes:

Continuous Market Research: Ongoing analysis of market trends, consumer behavior, and competitive dynamics provides insights for timely adjustments to product and marketing strategies.

Innovation and Adaptation: Proactively innovating and adapting product features, marketing messages, and strategies ensure relevance and competitiveness across all life cycle stages.

Portfolio Management: Balancing the product portfolio to include products at different life cycle stages mitigates risks and stabilizes revenue streams.

8.2 BUILDING AND SUSTAINING BRAND EQUITY

Brand equity, the value derived from consumer perception of a brand, is a crucial asset for companies aiming to establish a strong market presence and achieve long-term success. This sub-chapter delves into the strategic imperatives for building and sustaining brand equity, highlighting the role of consistent brand messaging, quality product offerings, and engaging customer experiences in fostering a positive brand image and loyalty.

Foundations of Brand Equity

Brand equity is built on three foundational pillars: brand awareness, brand associations, and brand loyalty. Each plays a pivotal role in how a brand is perceived in the minds of consumers and, consequently, in the marketplace.

Brand Awareness: The extent to which consumers are familiar with the brand and its products. High brand awareness is a precursor to building brand equity, as recognition is the first step in consumer decision-making.

Brand Associations: The thoughts, feelings, perceptions, and attitudes that consumers associate with a brand. Strong, positive brand associations are built through consistent marketing messages, quality products, and memorable brand experiences.

Brand Loyalty: The commitment of consumers to repeatedly purchase a brand's products over alternatives. Brand loyalty is the ultimate indicator of strong brand equity, reflecting a deep emotional connection and trust in the brand.

Strategies for Building Brand Equity

Building brand equity requires a strategic approach that integrates marketing, product development, and customer service to deliver a consistent and compelling brand promise.

Consistency in Brand Messaging: Ensure all marketing communications across various channels are aligned with the brand's core values and message. Consistency reinforces brand identity and aids in building strong associations.

Quality and Innovation in Product Offerings: Continuously offer high-quality products that meet or exceed customer expectations. Innovation keeps the brand relevant and allows it to set trends in the market.

Exceptional Customer Experiences: Deliver engaging and personalized experiences across all touchpoints. Positive experiences build emotional connections and encourage word-of-mouth promotion.

Leverage Digital Platforms: Utilize social media and online platforms to engage with consumers directly. Digital engagement allows for personalization and real-time feedback, enhancing brand perception.

Sustaining Brand Equity

Sustaining brand equity over time demands ongoing attention to consumer trends, market dynamics, and competitive actions. It requires a commitment to maintaining the quality and relevance of the brand's offerings.

Continuous Market Research: Stay informed about changing consumer preferences and market trends to adapt strategies accordingly and keep the brand aligned with consumer needs.

Adapt and Innovate: Be prepared to evolve the brand's offerings and messaging to stay ahead of market changes and technological advancements. Innovation should be at the heart of the brand's strategy to sustain its market position.

Foster Brand Advocacy: Encourage satisfied customers to become brand advocates. User-generated content, reviews, and testimonials can be powerful tools for building trust and sustaining brand equity.

Monitor Brand Health: Regularly assess brand equity through surveys, social listening, and market analysis. Monitoring allows for the identification of potential issues early on and the implementation of corrective measures.

8.3 BRAND MANAGEMENT IN THE DIGITAL AGE

Brand Management in the Digital Age

The advent of the digital age has transformed brand management, introducing both opportunities and challenges that necessitate a reevaluation of traditional strategies. In today's interconnected world, digital platforms have become pivotal in shaping consumer perceptions, interactions, and experiences with brands. This sub-chapter explores the critical aspects of brand management in the digital age, focusing on the strategies that businesses can employ to navigate the complexities of digital channels and maintain brand integrity and equity.

Digital Transformation of Brand Management

The digital transformation has extended brand management beyond traditional media and physical interactions, incorporating a vast array of digital touchpoints including social media, websites, mobile apps, and online communities. This shift requires brands to adopt a more dynamic and responsive approach to manage their online presence and engage with consumers.

Key Strategies for Digital Brand Management

Consistent Brand Identity Across Channels: Ensure that the brand's visual identity and messaging are consistent across all digital platforms. Uniformity reinforces brand recognition and aids in building a cohesive brand image.

Engagement Through Social Media: Social media platforms offer unique opportunities for brands to engage directly with consumers. Active participation, timely responses to inquiries and feedback, and engaging content creation are essential for fostering community and loyalty.

Leveraging Data for Personalization: Digital channels generate vast amounts of data that can be analyzed to gain insights into consumer behavior and preferences. Utilize this data to personalize marketing messages, offers, and experiences, enhancing relevance and connection with the audience.

Managing Online Reputation: Online reviews and social media comments play a significant role in shaping brand perception. Implement strategies for monitoring and responding to online feedback, addressing negative comments constructively, and highlighting positive testimonials.

Content Marketing: Develop and distribute valuable, relevant, and consistent content to attract and retain a clearly defined audience. Effective content marketing not only drives engagement but also establishes the brand as a thought leader in its industry.

SEO and Online Visibility: Implement search engine optimization (SEO) strategies to improve the brand's online visibility. High search rankings enhance credibility and can significantly impact brand awareness and perception.

Challenges in Digital Brand Management

Managing a brand in the digital age comes with its set of challenges, including:

Rapid Pace of Change: The digital landscape is constantly evolving, requiring brands to stay abreast of the latest trends, technologies, and consumer behaviors.

Increased Competition: Digital platforms lower entry barriers, intensifying competition and making it harder for brands to stand out.

Risk of Negative Exposure: The viral nature of digital content can amplify negative feedback or crises, posing risks to brand reputation.

Data Privacy and Security: With the increasing use of consumer data for personalization, brands must navigate the complexities of data privacy regulations and ensure the security of consumer information.

8.4 STRATEGIC CO-BRANDING AND PARTNERSHIPS

In an increasingly competitive market landscape, strategic co-branding and partnerships have emerged as powerful tools for businesses seeking to expand their reach, innovate their offerings, and enhance their brand equity. By aligning with complementary brands or entities, companies can leverage synergies, share resources, and tap into new customer bases. This sub-chapter explores the concept of strategic co-branding and partnerships, outlining their benefits, challenges, and key considerations for successful implementation.

Understanding Co-Branding and Partnerships

Co-branding involves a strategic collaboration between two or more brands to create a product or service that leverages the strength and market positioning of each partner. Similarly, strategic partnerships may encompass broader collaborations that extend beyond product offerings, including joint marketing campaigns, technology sharing, or distribution agreements.

Benefits of Co-Branding and Partnerships

Expanded Market Reach: Collaborations allow brands to access each other's customer bases, providing opportunities to reach and engage new segments.

Enhanced Brand Perception: Association with another reputable brand can elevate a company's brand image, enhancing perceived value and trust among consumers.

Resource Efficiency: Partnerships enable companies to share costs and resources, making it more efficient to explore new markets or develop innovative products.

Innovation Through Collaboration: Combining expertise and resources can foster innovation, leading to the development of unique products or services that differentiate the partners from competitors.

Key Strategies for Successful Co-Branding and Partnerships

Aligning Brand Values and Objectives: Successful collaborations are built on a foundation of aligned values and objectives. Partners should share a common vision for the partnership and how it will benefit both parties and their customers.

Careful Selection of Partners: Choosing the right partner is crucial. Brands should seek partners with complementary strengths, reputations, and market positions that can enhance the collaboration's value.

Clear Communication and Expectations: Establish clear lines of communication and set explicit expectations regarding roles, contributions, and outcomes. Transparency and regular dialogue help prevent misunderstandings and align efforts.

Joint Marketing and Promotion: Develop integrated marketing strategies that leverage the strengths of each partner. Coordinated promotional efforts can amplify the reach and impact of the partnership.

Monitoring and Evaluation: Continuously monitor the partnership's performance against predefined metrics. Regular evaluation enables partners to adjust strategies and optimize the collaboration's effectiveness.

Challenges in Co-Branding and Partnerships

While co-branding and partnerships offer significant benefits, they also present challenges:

Brand Dilution: There is a risk that collaborating with another brand could dilute or confuse the brand identity if not managed carefully.

Conflict of Interest: Diverging priorities or business objectives between partners can lead to conflicts, undermining the collaboration.

Customer Reception: The success of co-branded products or joint campaigns heavily depends on customer reception, which can be unpredictable.

CHAPTER 9. PRICING: STRATEGIES AND APPROACHES

In the intricate landscape of marketing, the formulation of pricing strategies stands as a critical determinant of a business's market success and financial sustainability. Pricing is not merely a reflection of the cost or value of a product or service but a complex decision that intersects with consumer psychology, competitive positioning, and market dynamics. This chapter delves into the art and science of pricing, exploring the myriad strategies and approaches that businesses can employ to optimize revenue, enhance customer value, and navigate the competitive marketplace effectively.

The journey of establishing a pricing strategy begins with a thorough analysis of various influencing factors. Central to these considerations are the cost of goods sold (COGS) and operational expenses, which form the baseline for ensuring profitability. Beyond costs, the perceived value of a product or service by target consumers plays a pivotal role, guiding value-based pricing strategies that align price points with customer expectations and willingness to pay. Market demand elasticity further informs pricing, requiring businesses to gauge how price adjustments might impact consumer purchase behavior and overall demand.

In parallel, understanding the competitive landscape is indispensable. Competitor pricing and market positioning offer critical benchmarks, influencing whether a business adopts a strategy of price leadership, penetration, or skimming. Regulatory frameworks and economic conditions also weigh in, especially in industries subject to price controls or those significantly affected by economic cycles.

Diverse pricing models and strategies offer businesses a spectrum of options for aligning their offerings with market and consumer realities. Cost-plus pricing provides a straightforward approach, adding a standard markup to costs to ensure profitability. In contrast, value-based pricing takes a more nuanced approach, setting prices according to the perceived worth of a product or service to the consumer, often leading to higher margins and enhanced brand value.

Competitive and penetration pricing strategies are employed to navigate market entry and positioning challenges, with the former focusing on aligning with or undercutting competitor prices, and the latter on low initial pricing to gain market share rapidly. Price skimming, conversely, targets segments willing to pay a premium at launch, capturing maximum revenue before gradually lowering prices to capture additional market segments.

The digital age has introduced dynamic and personalized pricing, leveraging real-time data and analytics to adjust prices based on market demand, inventory levels, or consumer profiles. While offering opportunities for revenue optimization, these approaches necessitate careful management to avoid consumer backlash or perceptions of unfairness.

E-commerce and online marketplaces further complicate the pricing landscape, introducing transparency that enables consumers to easily compare prices across vendors. Online pricing strategies must thus consider the ease of price comparison, employing promotional pricing, discounts, and dynamic pricing tactics to attract and retain customers. The freemium model, offering basic services for free while charging for advanced features, exemplifies innovative online pricing that can drive user base expansion and upsell opportunities.

9.1 ANALYZING FACTORS THAT INFLUENCE PRICING

In the complex realm of market dynamics, pricing stands as one of the most pivotal elements influencing consumer decision-making and business profitability. Understanding and analyzing the factors that influence pricing is crucial for businesses aiming to establish effective pricing strategies that resonate with consumers and ensure competitive advantage. This section delves into the myriad of factors that businesses must consider to navigate the intricacies of pricing decisions.

Cost Structure: A foundational factor in pricing is the cost structure of the product or service, encompassing both the direct costs associated with production and indirect costs such as overhead. Understanding the total cost of goods sold (COGS) is essential for setting a price point that ensures profitability while remaining competitive in the market.

Consumer Perceptions of Value: How consumers perceive the value of a product or service significantly influences pricing power. Value-based pricing strategies hinge on aligning price points with the perceived benefits and differentiation of the offering in the eyes of the target market. This requires a deep understanding of consumer needs, preferences, and willingness to pay.

Market Demand and Elasticity: The demand for a product and its price elasticity—how sensitive demand is to changes in price—play critical roles in pricing decisions. Products with inelastic demand can often command higher prices, while those with elastic demand require more strategic pricing to balance volume and profitability.

Competitive Landscape: The pricing strategies of competitors in the market are a crucial consideration. Analyzing competitive price points and value propositions helps businesses position their offerings strategically, whether by matching, undercutting, or premium pricing to differentiate from the competition.

Brand Positioning: The positioning of a brand within its market and the equity it holds influence pricing capabilities. Premium brands with strong brand equity can often command higher prices based on their perceived value and reputation.

Regulatory and Legal Considerations: In certain industries, regulatory and legal factors may dictate pricing boundaries. Compliance with pricing regulations and consideration of legal constraints are essential to avoid potential sanctions or market restrictions.

Distribution Channels: The choice of distribution channels also impacts pricing strategies. Different channels may entail varied costs and margin requirements, influencing the final price to the consumer. Additionally, channel partners may have pricing expectations or restrictions that need to be considered.

Economic Conditions: Broader economic factors, including inflation rates, currency fluctuations, and overall economic health, can affect pricing strategies. Businesses must adapt their pricing to reflect economic realities and consumer purchasing power.

Technological Advancements: Technological changes can influence production costs, consumer expectations, and competitive dynamics, all of which impact pricing decisions. Staying abreast of technological trends is crucial for maintaining competitive pricing strategies.

9.2 EXPLORING DIVERSE PRICING MODELS AND STRATEGIES

In the competitive landscape of modern business, adopting a nuanced approach to pricing is crucial for success. Diverse pricing models and strategies enable businesses to cater to a broad spectrum of consumer preferences, adapt to market dynamics, and optimize revenue streams. This exploration sheds light on the various pricing models and strategies at the disposal of businesses, each with its unique advantages and applications.

1. Cost-Plus Pricing: This straightforward model involves adding a fixed margin to the cost of producing a product or service. While simple to implement, it may not always reflect the product's market value or consumer willingness to pay.

2. Value-Based Pricing: This strategy sets prices primarily on the perceived value to the customer rather than the cost of production. It requires a deep understanding of the target market's needs and preferences, allowing businesses to charge a premium for products that offer unique benefits or solve specific problems.

3. Competitive Pricing: Also known as market-oriented pricing, this approach involves setting prices based on competitors' pricing strategies. Companies may choose to price their products slightly lower, at parity, or higher than competitors, depending on their market positioning and brand value.

4. Penetration Pricing: Aimed at quickly capturing market share, penetration pricing involves setting lower prices for new products to attract customers from competitors. Although it can lead to initial losses, it's effective for building a customer base in highly competitive markets.

5. Price Skimming: This strategy involves setting high initial prices for new or innovative products to maximize revenue from early adopters. Over time, prices are gradually lowered to attract more price-sensitive segments of the market.

6. Psychological Pricing: Leveraging consumer psychology, this approach includes tactics like pricing products just below a round number (e.g., $9.99 instead of $10) to make the price appear significantly lower. It plays on consumer perceptions to drive sales.

7. Bundle Pricing: By offering a group of products or services together at a lower price than they would cost individually, businesses can encourage the purchase of more items and increase the overall transaction value.

8. Freemium Pricing: Common in digital products and services, the freemium model offers basic features for free while charging for premium or advanced features. This strategy is designed to attract a large user base and convert a portion to paying customers.

9. Dynamic Pricing: Utilizing algorithms and market data, dynamic pricing adjusts prices in real-time based on demand, competitor prices, and other market factors. It's widely used in industries like hospitality, travel, and e-commerce.

10. Subscription Pricing: This model charges customers a recurring fee to access a product or service. Subscription pricing ensures a steady revenue stream and can build customer loyalty over time.

Challenges and Considerations:

Adopting these pricing strategies requires careful consideration of the market context, consumer behavior, and competitive landscape. Businesses must also be mindful of the potential impacts on brand perception and customer loyalty. Moreover, regulatory and ethical considerations are paramount, especially in strategies like dynamic pricing, where there is a risk of perceived price gouging.

9.3 DYNAMIC AND PERSONALIZED PRICING

In the era of digital transformation, dynamic and personalized pricing strategies have emerged as innovative approaches to optimize revenue and enhance customer engagement. By leveraging data analytics, artificial intelligence (AI), and real-time market insights, businesses can adjust prices dynamically and offer personalized pricing to individual customers. This section explores the mechanisms, benefits, and ethical considerations of these advanced pricing strategies.

Dynamic Pricing

Dynamic pricing, also known as surge pricing or demand pricing, is a strategy where prices are adjusted in real-time based on current market demand, inventory levels, competitor pricing, and other external factors. Widely adopted in industries such as airlines, hospitality, and e-commerce, dynamic pricing allows businesses to maximize profitability by capitalizing on market fluctuations.

Mechanisms of Dynamic Pricing:

Market Demand: Prices increase during peak demand periods and decrease when demand wanes.

Competitor Pricing: Prices are adjusted in response to changes in competitors' pricing strategies.

Inventory Levels: Prices are optimized based on inventory availability to balance supply and demand.

Benefits of Dynamic Pricing:

Revenue Optimization: By adjusting prices based on demand, businesses can maximize revenue during peak periods and stimulate sales during off-peak times.

Market Responsiveness: Dynamic pricing enables businesses to quickly respond to market changes, maintaining competitiveness.

Efficient Inventory Management: Strategically adjusting prices based on inventory helps in clearing stock and reducing overstock.

Personalized Pricing

Personalized pricing takes customization a step further by offering individualized prices based on customer-specific data, such as purchase history, browsing behavior, and customer loyalty. This approach aims to maximize the value exchange between the business and each customer, enhancing customer satisfaction and loyalty.

Mechanisms of Personalized Pricing:

Customer Data Analysis: Leveraging data analytics to understand individual customer behavior and willingness to pay.

Segmentation: Identifying customer segments with similar characteristics to tailor pricing strategies effectively.

AI and Machine Learning: Using AI algorithms to predict optimal pricing for individual customers or segments in real-time.

Benefits of Personalized Pricing:

Increased Customer Engagement: Personalized pricing can enhance the customer experience by offering deals and prices that match individual preferences.

Revenue and Profitability Growth: By aligning price points with customer willingness to pay, businesses can optimize revenue and margins.

Competitive Differentiation: Offering personalized prices can differentiate a brand in a crowded market, fostering customer loyalty.

Ethical Considerations and Challenges:

Transparency and Fairness: There is a delicate balance between personalization and perceived price discrimination. Businesses must navigate ethical considerations, ensuring transparency and fairness to maintain customer trust.

Privacy Concerns: Personalized pricing relies on collecting and analyzing customer data, raising concerns about data privacy and security. Adhering to data protection regulations and ethical standards is paramount.

Implementation Complexity: Both dynamic and personalized pricing require sophisticated technology and analytics capabilities, which can be resource-intensive to implement and manage.

9.4 E-COMMERCE AND ONLINE PRICING STRATEGIES

The digital marketplace has revolutionized the way businesses approach pricing strategies. E-commerce and online platforms offer unique opportunities for dynamic and competitive pricing, but they also introduce challenges related to consumer perception and market saturation. This section explores the intricacies of e-commerce and online pricing strategies, highlighting approaches that businesses can utilize to optimize their online sales and maintain competitive advantage.

Key Strategies for E-Commerce Pricing

Dynamic Pricing: Leveraging the power of online platforms, businesses can implement dynamic pricing strategies, adjusting prices in real-time based on demand, competition, and other market factors. This flexibility allows e-commerce businesses to respond quickly to market changes, optimizing profitability.

Psychological Pricing: Online environments are ideal for deploying psychological pricing tactics, such as charm pricing (e.g., pricing items at $9.99 instead of $10). These strategies play on consumer psychology to make prices appear more attractive, potentially boosting sales.

Price Discrimination: E-commerce platforms can utilize customer data to offer personalized pricing, although this strategy must be approached with caution due to ethical and legal considerations. Price discrimination can involve offering discounts to first-time visitors or providing exclusive offers to loyalty program members.

Freemium Models: Particularly common in digital services and software, the freemium model offers basic services for free while charging for premium features. This strategy can attract a broad user base, with the potential to upsell premium services to a segment of those users.

Competitive Pricing Analysis: Online tools and algorithms enable businesses to conduct real-time competitive pricing analysis, allowing them to adjust their prices to stay competitive within the market. This strategy requires continuous monitoring to ensure pricing remains optimal in relation to competitors.

Discounts and Promotions: Flash sales, seasonal discounts, and exclusive promotions can drive traffic and conversions on e-commerce platforms. These strategies can be used to clear inventory, attract new customers, or reward loyal ones.

Value-Based Pricing: Even in the competitive online marketplace, businesses can successfully implement value-based pricing by clearly communicating the unique value and benefits of their products or services. This approach focuses on aligning prices with the perceived value to the customer, rather than solely competing on price.

Challenges in Online Pricing

Price Transparency: The transparency of the internet makes it easy for consumers to compare prices, necessitating strategic pricing to ensure competitiveness without eroding profit margins.

Consumer Sensitivity to Price Changes: Frequent price changes can lead to consumer distrust. Businesses must balance dynamic pricing strategies with the need to maintain consumer trust.

Global Competition: E-commerce opens up global markets, introducing competition not only from local businesses but from international sellers as well, complicating pricing strategies.

CHAPTER 10. CHANNELS AND LOGISTICS: DISTRIBUTION AND SUPPLY CHAIN MANAGEMENT

In the intricate world of marketing, the mastery of distribution channels and logistics forms the bedrock of ensuring that products not only reach consumers in the most efficient, cost-effective, and timely manner but also stand out in a fiercely competitive marketplace. The chapter on "Channels and Logistics: Distribution and Supply Chain Management" embarks on a detailed exploration of the fundamental aspects that govern the effective distribution and management of supply chains, emphasizing the critical role these elements play in amplifying product accessibility, optimizing inventory levels, and, most importantly, heightening customer satisfaction and loyalty.

At the core of this discussion lies the essence of distribution channels, which act as vital conduits through which goods and services traverse from producers to the end consumers. This network of pathways, encompassing a diverse array of intermediaries such as wholesalers, retailers, distributors, and e-commerce platforms, is chosen through a strategic lens influenced by various factors including product nature, target market preferences, and the prevailing competitive dynamics. Effective management of these channels ensures widespread market coverage, bolsters brand visibility, and guarantees the prompt delivery of products to consumers.

Further, the chapter intertwines logistics and supply chain management with distribution, spotlighting the behind-the-scenes operations essential for moving products from production sites to consumers. This includes a detailed look into transportation, warehousing, inventory management, order fulfillment, and the complexities of returns management. Strategic planning in logistics is highlighted as crucial for reducing costs, maximizing operational efficiency, and maintaining the flexibility needed to respond to market demands or supply chain disruptions swiftly.

The transformative power of technology on distribution and logistics is also dissected, revealing how advancements have led to more sophisticated supply chain analytics, real-time tracking, and automated inventory management systems. The narrative acknowledges the revolutionary impact of e-commerce platforms, which have shifted focus towards digital channels and direct-to-consumer models, necessitating adaptations in logistics operations to prioritize speed, flexibility, and precision in order fulfillment.

Challenges within distribution and supply chain management are discussed, from navigating multi-channel distribution strategies and ensuring sustainability in logistics operations to mitigating risks related to supply chain disruptions. The chapter closes by addressing the increasing importance of sustainability and ethical considerations in distribution and supply chain management, with a call to action for implementing practices that not only enhance brand reputation but also contribute significantly to environmental stewardship.

10.1 MAPPING OUT DISTRIBUTION CHANNELS

Mapping out distribution channels is a strategic process that involves identifying and selecting the pathways through which products or services move from the manufacturer to the end consumer. This crucial step in supply chain management not only determines how goods are delivered but also significantly impacts a company's market reach, customer satisfaction, and overall profitability. Effective channel mapping requires a deep understanding of the market, consumer preferences, and the unique characteristics of the product or service being offered.

Types of Distribution Channels

Distribution channels can be direct or indirect, each with its advantages and challenges:

Direct Channels involve the manufacturer selling directly to the consumer without intermediaries. This could be through company-owned stores, e-commerce websites, or direct mail. Direct channels offer greater control over the customer experience and potentially higher margins but require significant investment in infrastructure and customer service operations.

Indirect Channels involve intermediaries such as wholesalers, distributors, retailers, or agents who facilitate the movement of goods from the manufacturer to the consumer. Indirect channels can expand market reach and leverage the expertise of channel partners but may reduce profit margins and lessen control over the brand experience.

Factors Influencing Channel Selection

Several factors influence the selection of distribution channels, including:

Product Characteristics: The nature of the product, including its perishability, complexity, and value, can dictate suitable distribution channels. High-value or highly technical products may benefit from direct channels that offer detailed customer support, while widely used consumer goods may thrive in indirect channels with broad distribution.

Market Considerations: Understanding the target market, including consumer buying behavior and preferred shopping channels, is critical. Products targeting tech-savvy consumers may prioritize online channels, whereas goods appealing to a more traditional demographic might focus on brick-and-mortar retailers.

Competitive Landscape: The distribution strategies of competitors can influence channel selection. Companies may choose to differentiate by using alternative channels or compete directly in established channels.

Cost and Efficiency: The cost-effectiveness and operational efficiency of different channels are significant considerations. Companies must balance the desire for market coverage with the need to maintain manageable costs and efficient logistics.

Strategies for Effective Channel Management

Partner Relationships: Building strong relationships with channel partners is key to effective distribution. This includes clear communication of goals, collaborative marketing efforts, and mutual support to enhance sales and customer satisfaction.

Channel Integration: For companies utilizing multiple distribution channels, ensuring a seamless and integrated customer experience across channels is paramount. This might involve consistent branding, pricing strategies, and customer service standards.

Monitoring and Adaptation: Continuously monitoring the performance of distribution channels and being prepared to adapt strategies in response to market changes, technological advancements, or shifts in consumer preferences is essential for long-term success.

10.2 LOGISTICS AND SUPPLY CHAIN DYNAMICS IN MARKETING

Logistics and supply chain dynamics play a pivotal role in the marketing strategy of any business, directly impacting product availability, customer satisfaction, and competitive advantage. The seamless integration of logistics and supply chain operations with marketing efforts ensures that products not only meet but exceed customer expectations, fostering brand loyalty and driving sales growth. This exploration delves into the intricate relationship between logistics, supply chain management, and marketing, highlighting how strategic alignment among these areas can propel a business forward.

The Intersection of Logistics and Marketing

At its core, logistics focuses on the efficient and effective transportation and storage of goods from point of origin to point of consumption. Supply chain management, encompassing a broader scope, involves coordinating and optimizing all activities involved in sourcing, procurement, conversion, and logistics management. When aligned with marketing strategies, logistics and supply chain dynamics can significantly enhance customer value propositions by ensuring product availability, maintaining quality, and optimizing costs.

Enhancing Customer Value through Supply Chain Excellence

Timely Delivery: Meeting or exceeding delivery expectations is crucial for customer satisfaction and retention. Efficient logistics operations, including advanced planning, route optimization, and real-time tracking, enable businesses to provide reliable and prompt delivery services, a critical component of the overall marketing promise.

Product Availability: Effective supply chain management ensures that products are available where and when customers want them, minimizing stockouts and optimizing inventory levels across distribution points. This reliability strengthens brand reputation and supports marketing claims of superior customer service.

Cost Optimization: Streamlined logistics and supply chain processes can significantly reduce operational costs, savings that can be passed on to customers in the form of competitive pricing or reinvested in marketing campaigns to drive brand differentiation and value.

Customization and Personalization: Advanced logistics and supply chain solutions facilitate product customization and personalization, catering to individual customer preferences. This capability can be a powerful marketing tool, differentiating a brand in a crowded market.

Challenges at the Nexus of Logistics, Supply Chain, and Marketing

Aligning Objectives: Bridging the gap between logistics/supply chain efficiency and marketing goals requires strategic alignment across departments, ensuring that operational capabilities support marketing promises.

Adapting to Market Demands: Rapid changes in consumer preferences and market conditions demand agile supply chain and logistics responses. Balancing flexibility with efficiency poses a significant challenge.

Sustainability and Ethics: Consumers are increasingly valuing sustainability and ethical practices in their purchasing decisions. Integrating sustainable logistics and supply chain practices is not only a marketing advantage but also a business imperative.

Strategies for Integrating Logistics and Marketing

Cross-Functional Teams: Creating cross-functional teams that include members from logistics, supply chain, and marketing can foster better alignment of strategies and objectives, enhancing overall business performance.

Technology Integration: Leveraging technology such as AI, IoT, and blockchain can enhance supply chain visibility, improve logistics efficiency, and provide data for targeted marketing strategies.

Customer Feedback Loops: Implementing systems to gather and analyze customer feedback related to delivery and product quality can inform both supply chain improvements and marketing strategies.

10.3 E-COMMERCE'S IMPACT ON DISTRIBUTION

The rise of e-commerce has fundamentally transformed the landscape of distribution, reshaping how products are stored, sold, and delivered to consumers. This digital revolution has not only expanded market reach for businesses of all sizes but also introduced new challenges and opportunities in logistics and supply chain management. This section examines the profound impact of e-commerce on distribution channels, logistics operations, and consumer expectations, highlighting the strategic shifts businesses must navigate to thrive in the digital marketplace.

Expansion of Direct-to-Consumer Channels

E-commerce has enabled businesses to bypass traditional intermediaries, facilitating direct-to-consumer (DTC) sales. This shift towards DTC channels offers businesses greater control over the customer experience, from marketing and sales to post-purchase support. However, it also necessitates investments in logistics infrastructure, such as warehousing and fulfillment centers, and sophisticated e-commerce platforms to manage online transactions.

Increased Demand for Speed and Flexibility

Consumer expectations for rapid delivery have escalated in the e-commerce era, with same-day and next-day delivery becoming increasingly standard. This demand for speed has driven innovations in logistics and distribution, including the adoption of advanced inventory management systems, the establishment of strategically located distribution centers, and the use of AI and data analytics for route optimization. Companies must now balance the need for fast, flexible delivery options with cost considerations and operational efficiency.

Challenges in Last-Mile Delivery

Last-mile delivery, the final step in the delivery process to the customer's doorstep, presents significant challenges in e-commerce distribution. Urban congestion, rural accessibility, and the environmental impact of delivery operations are critical issues businesses must address. Solutions such as localized fulfillment centers, partnerships with third-party logistics providers, and investments in eco-friendly delivery options are being explored to enhance last-mile efficiency.

Return Logistics Complexity

E-commerce has also led to a surge in product returns, adding complexity to distribution and logistics operations. Efficient handling of returns, including reverse logistics processes for collecting, processing, and restocking returned items, is crucial for maintaining customer satisfaction and minimizing losses. This has prompted businesses to invest in return management systems and to consider returns as a key component of the customer experience.

Global Market Access

The digital marketplace has opened global sales opportunities for businesses, allowing them to reach customers across borders with relative ease. However, this expansion requires navigating international logistics, including customs, tariffs, and varying consumer regulations. Effective e-commerce distribution on a global scale demands robust international logistics partnerships and a deep understanding of local market dynamics.

Adapting to Technological Advancements

E-commerce distribution is continuously evolving, driven by technological advancements. From drone deliveries and autonomous vehicles to blockchain for supply chain transparency, businesses must stay abreast of emerging technologies to remain competitive. Investing in innovation and adapting logistics strategies to incorporate new technologies are key for businesses looking to leverage e-commerce's full potential.

Twitch's remarkable journey in building a vibrant and engaged community provides a compelling case study on effective digital brand management. This story is a testament to how Twitch harnessed the power of live streaming and community engagement to create a unique space for gamers and content creators alike.

The Core of Twitch's Strategy

Twitch's success is rooted in its understanding of the gaming community's desire for live, interactive content. Unlike platforms that rely on pre-recorded videos, Twitch focuses on live video streaming, creating a real-time connection between streamers and their audiences. This approach fosters a sense of immediacy and authenticity, key factors in building strong community ties. Streamers like SypherPK have highlighted the importance of regular live streaming in establishing personal connections with viewers at a faster pace than other platforms allow.

Building and Fostering Community Engagement

One of Twitch's standout strategies is encouraging streamers to engage with their audience actively. This includes acknowledging new subscribers by name, hosting and raiding other streamers to promote a sense of camaraderie, and leveraging social media to promote channels. Moreover, Twitch streamers often collaborate on events, which further strengthens the community bond and increases viewer engagement across channels.

Promotional strategies are also crucial. Streamers use social media platforms to announce stream schedules and share content highlights, attracting new viewers. Additionally, creating compelling trailers and clips helps capture the audience's attention, showcasing the best moments and what new viewers can expect.

Partnering with Brands

Twitch's ecosystem offers unique opportunities for brand partnerships. Streamers carefully select brands that resonate with their audience, ensuring that promotional content is relevant and engaging. Live interactions on Twitch allow for creative promotional content, where streamers can instantly gauge audience response, creating a buzz around products or campaigns in real-time. This level of engagement is invaluable for brands looking to tap into dedicated and passionate communities.

The Future of Livestreaming

The future of livestreaming, with Twitch at the forefront, promises even greater integration into our daily lives. As the platform continues to evolve, offering diverse content categories, the opportunities for brands to engage with specific communities will expand. This evolution underscores the potential of live audience interaction in creating more creative and impactful brand integrations.

Twitch's approach to community building—centered on live engagement, content quality, and strategic brand partnerships—highlights the platform's unique position in the digital landscape. By fostering a space where streamers and viewers form genuine connections, Twitch has not only revolutionized how content is consumed but has also set a new standard for digital community engagement.

PART III: ADVANCED MARKETING PRACTICES AND DIGITAL INTEGRATION

Nike's 'Breaking2' Campaign

(AI Generated Photo)

Nike's "Breaking2" campaign in 2017 was a groundbreaking marketing effort that combined sports, science, and storytelling. The campaign's goal was to break the two-hour barrier for the marathon, a feat never before achieved. Nike sponsored three elite runners, Eliud Kipchoge, Lelisa Desisa, and Zersenay Tadese, in this endeavor.

The attempt to break the two-hour marathon was live-streamed globally, allowing audiences worldwide to witness history in the making. The campaign included extensive behind-the-scenes content, athlete stories, and technological innovations used to enhance performance. Though the two-hour barrier was not broken, with Kipchoge finishing in 2:00:25, the campaign was a massive success in terms of audience engagement and brand enhancement for Nike.

"Breaking2" showcased Nike's commitment to innovation and excellence, resonating deeply with both professional and amateur athletes. It also highlighted the power of digital marketing in creating a globally engaging and immersive experience.

CHAPTER 11. INTEGRATED MARKETING COMMUNICATION TECHNIQUES

In the swiftly evolving digital landscape, the chapter on Integrated Marketing Communication Techniques explores the fusion of various promotional tools and channels to deliver a unified, coherent, and compelling brand message. This strategic approach is critical in today's fragmented media environment, ensuring that a brand's narrative is consistent across all platforms, from traditional advertising and public relations to the dynamic realms of social media and influencer marketing. The chapter underscores the importance of harmonizing advertising and public relations (PR), leveraging their unique strengths to craft a resonant brand story. As advertising evolves to include digital formats like online ads and social media, it becomes more targeted and interactive, emphasizing engagement over mere reach. Similarly, PR has adapted to the digital age, utilizing social media and other direct channels to manage brand image and engage with stakeholders in real time.

Sales promotions and personal selling are highlighted as key strategies for enhancing brand impact and achieving immediate sales goals. Sales promotions, such as discounts and limited-time offers, create urgency and incentivize consumer action. Personal selling, on the other hand, builds one-on-one relationships, addressing specific customer needs and preferences. The chapter also delves into the critical role of social media and influencers in modern marketing strategies. Social media platforms offer brands spaces to interact with their audience, fostering community and engagement. Influencer marketing, leveraging the trust influencers have built with their followers, allows brands to convey their messages more authentically and effectively.

Finally, the integration of traditional and digital media is discussed as a pivotal evolution in marketing communication. This blend combines the reach and credibility of traditional media with the precision and interactivity of digital channels, amplifying a brand's message across diverse audience segments. Through strategic integration and examples like Oreo's "Dunk in the Dark" campaign, the chapter illustrates the power of a well-orchestrated mix of media in achieving marketing success

11.1 THE DYNAMICS OF ADVERTISING AND PUBLIC RELATIONS

In the realm of Integrated Marketing Communications (IMC), the synergy between advertising and public relations (PR) forms the backbone of a brand's ability to engage its audience compellingly and cohesively. This synergy is not merely about coordinating messages but about leveraging the unique strengths of each discipline to build a brand narrative that resonates deeply with consumers. Understanding the dynamics of advertising and PR, and how they can be harmonized, is essential for marketers aiming to navigate the complex media landscape of today effectively.

The Evolution of Advertising

Advertising has undergone a transformative evolution from its traditional forms—such as television commercials, print ads, and billboards—to include a vast array of digital formats, including online display ads, search engine marketing, and social media ads. This evolution is characterized by a shift towards more personalized, targeted, and interactive formats, enabled by digital technology and data analytics. For instance, programmatic advertising uses algorithms to purchase ad space in real time, allowing for more precise targeting and optimization of ad spend based on user behavior and preferences.

Digital platforms have also introduced new models of engagement, where the effectiveness of an ad is not just measured by its reach but by the interaction it generates among the audience. This shift emphasizes the importance of creating content that resonates with the audience, encouraging them to engage with the brand beyond the ad itself.

The Strategic Role of Public Relations

While advertising focuses on paid media to promote products or services directly, PR primarily operates in the realm of earned media, aiming to build and maintain a positive image of the brand among its stakeholders. This involves managing communication with the media, influencers, and directly with the public through social media and other channels. Effective PR strategies can enhance a brand's credibility and trustworthiness, as positive media coverage and word-of-mouth recommendations are often perceived as more authentic than paid advertising.

The rise of digital media has expanded the toolkit available to PR professionals, enabling more direct and interactive forms of communication with the public. Social media, in particular, has become a critical platform for crisis management, allowing brands to respond quickly and publicly to any issues that may arise. Moreover, content marketing—a strategy that involves creating valuable, relevant content to attract and engage a defined audience—has blurred the lines between advertising and PR, as it often aims to both inform and promote.

Harmonizing Advertising and PR

The key to maximizing the impact of advertising and PR lies in their integration within a comprehensive IMC strategy. By ensuring that all messaging is consistent across both paid and earned media, brands can create a more unified and compelling narrative. This harmonization extends beyond the message itself to include the timing, channels, and audiences targeted by both advertising and PR efforts.

A notable example of this harmonization is Apple's product launch events, which combine the spectacle of advertising with the credibility of PR. By generating media buzz and leveraging social media to amplify its message, Apple creates a holistic marketing campaign that not only promotes its products but also reinforces its brand identity.

11.2 ENHANCING IMPACT THROUGH SALES PROMOTION AND PERSONAL SELLING

The landscape of marketing communications is vast and varied, with sales promotions and personal selling standing out as pivotal strategies for driving consumer engagement and achieving immediate sales objectives. While sales promotions aim to create a compelling incentive for consumers to make a purchase in the short term, personal selling focuses on building one-on-one relationships between salespeople and customers to understand and fulfill their needs more effectively. Both strategies are instrumental in enhancing the impact of a brand's marketing efforts, and when integrated within a broader marketing communication strategy, they can significantly boost overall campaign effectiveness.

Sales Promotion: Creating Urgency and Incentivizing Action

Sales promotions are diverse, including discounts, coupons, contests, and limited-time offers, designed to stimulate immediate interest and prompt action from consumers. By offering tangible benefits or exclusive opportunities, they can effectively interrupt the consumer's usual decision-making process, encouraging them to choose a particular brand or product now rather than later.

For example, Black Friday and Cyber Monday have become synonymous with significant discounts and are highly anticipated by consumers worldwide. Retailers and e-commerce platforms leverage these events to drive massive spikes in sales, using a combination of deep discounts, flash sales, and exclusive deals to create a sense of urgency and exclusivity.

Another innovative example of sales promotion is the "Buy One, Get One Free" (BOGOF) offer, which not only encourages purchase but also increases the perceived value of the offer, making it more difficult for the consumer to resist.

Personal Selling: Building Relationships and Tailoring Solutions

Personal selling is the most direct form of marketing communication, involving face-to-face interaction between a salesperson and a potential customer. This approach allows for a personalized experience, where the salesperson can adapt their pitch to address the specific needs, concerns, and preferences of the customer.

In industries where the products or services are complex, high-value, or require significant investment, personal selling becomes particularly important. For instance, in the B2B sector, sales representatives play a crucial role in educating customers about their offerings, negotiating terms, and providing post-sale support.

A notable example of effective personal selling is found in the pharmaceutical industry, where sales representatives, often referred to as "detailers," visit doctors and healthcare professionals to inform them about new medications. By providing valuable information and building relationships with healthcare providers, pharmaceutical companies can influence prescriptions and drive product adoption.

Integrating Sales Promotion and Personal Selling

The integration of sales promotion and personal selling strategies can lead to a more cohesive and impactful marketing communication effort. For example, a sales promotion can generate interest and bring potential customers into a store or onto a website, where personal selling techniques can then be employed to further educate the customer, address their concerns, and close the sale.

Car dealerships often employ this integrated approach effectively. Special promotions, such as zero percent financing or cash-back offers, attract customers to the dealership. Once there, skilled salespeople engage with the customers, using their insights and expertise to tailor the sales pitch, highlight the features and benefits of different vehicles, and ultimately guide the customer through the purchase decision.

11.3 ROLE OF SOCIAL MEDIA AND INFLUENCERS

In the digital era, social media and influencers have become pivotal elements of Integrated Marketing Communication (IMC) strategies, offering unparalleled opportunities for brands to engage with audiences in a direct, authentic, and interactive manner. The power of these platforms lies in their ability to humanize brands, foster community, and amplify messages through voices that consumers trust and follow. This section explores the transformative role of social media and influencers in contemporary marketing practices.

The Power of Social Media in Marketing

Social media platforms, such as Instagram, Facebook, Twitter, LinkedIn, and TikTok, provide brands with dynamic spaces to share content, interact with consumers, and participate in conversations. These platforms enable brands to not only broadcast their messages but also listen to and engage with their audiences, offering a level of interaction that traditional media cannot match. By leveraging the unique features of each platform—be it Instagram stories, Twitter hashtags, or TikTok challenges—brands can create diverse content strategies that resonate with their target demographics.

A notable example of social media's impact is the #ShareACoke campaign by Coca-Cola. By personalizing bottles with people's names and encouraging consumers to share their experiences on social media, Coca-Cola transformed a simple beverage purchase into a personal and shareable moment, significantly boosting brand engagement and consumer participation across platforms.

Influencer Marketing: Leveraging Trust and Authenticity

Influencer marketing capitalizes on the trust and rapport that influencers have built with their followers. By partnering with influencers whose audiences align with their target market, brands can convey their messages in a more authentic and relatable manner. Influencers, ranging from celebrities and industry experts to micro-influencers with niche followings, can offer endorsements, reviews, tutorials, and unique content collaborations, thereby influencing their followers' perceptions and buying behaviors.

A prime example of effective influencer marketing is the partnership between the beauty brand Glossier and a wide array of influencers. Glossier's strategy focuses on engaging with both high-profile personalities and micro-influencers who share genuine experiences with their products. This approach not only broadens their reach but also enhances the authenticity of their brand message, driving engagement and loyalty.

Integrating Social Media and Influencers into IMC

The integration of social media and influencers into an IMC strategy requires a thoughtful approach that aligns with the brand's overall objectives and messaging. Successful integration involves:

Choosing the Right Platforms and Influencers: Select platforms and influencers that best match the brand's target audience and values. This alignment ensures that the content resonates with the audience and feels natural within the influencer's usual content stream.

Creating Cohesive and Authentic Content: While consistency in messaging is crucial, it's equally important for content to remain authentic to both the brand's voice and the influencer's style. This balance enhances credibility and engagement.

Measuring and Optimizing: Utilizing social media analytics and influencer performance metrics allows brands to measure the effectiveness of their campaigns, enabling continuous optimization of strategies for better engagement and ROI.

11.4 BLENDING TRADITIONAL AND DIGITAL MEDIA

The convergence of traditional and digital media marks a pivotal evolution in the landscape of Integrated Marketing Communication (IMC). This blending harnesses the strengths of both worlds—combining the reach and tangibility of traditional media with the interactivity and precision of digital platforms. A well-orchestrated mix can amplify a brand's message, ensuring it resonates with diverse audience segments across multiple touchpoints. This section explores strategies for effectively merging traditional and digital media, along with illustrative examples of successful integration.

Leveraging the Strengths of Traditional Media

Traditional media—encompassing television, radio, print, and outdoor advertising—offers broad reach, high visibility, and in many cases, a sense of credibility that comes from being featured in established channels. These mediums excel in building brand awareness and delivering impactful messages that can leave a lasting impression. For example, television ads during major events like the Super Bowl have the power to reach millions of viewers simultaneously, creating significant brand moments that become part of cultural conversations.

Harnessing the Precision of Digital Media

Digital media, through channels like social media, email, search engines, and websites, offers unparalleled opportunities for targeting, engagement, and measurement. Brands can use digital platforms to deliver personalized messages to specific audience segments, engage in two-way conversations, and track the effectiveness of their campaigns in real time. The agility of digital media allows for quick adjustments based on performance data, optimizing the impact of marketing efforts.

Successful Integration of Traditional and Digital Media

Integrating traditional and digital media requires a strategic approach that aligns with overall marketing objectives and leverages the unique advantages of each medium. The following are key strategies for effective integration:

Creating Multi-Channel Campaigns: Design campaigns that span both traditional and digital channels, ensuring consistent messaging that's adapted to the strengths of each medium. For instance, a campaign might launch with a captivating TV commercial to build broad awareness, followed by targeted social media ads to engage specific consumer segments more deeply.

Utilizing Traditional Media to Amplify Digital Efforts: Traditional media can serve as a powerful driver to digital channels. QR codes in print ads, hashtags promoted in TV commercials, and radio mentions directing listeners to a website are examples of how traditional media can enhance digital engagement.

Leveraging Digital Insights to Inform Traditional Media Buys: Data from digital campaigns can provide valuable insights into audience behaviors and preferences, guiding more informed decisions in traditional media placements. This data-driven approach ensures that traditional media efforts are targeted more effectively, enhancing overall campaign efficiency.

Illustrative Example: The Oreo "Dunk in the Dark" Campaign

A quintessential example of blending traditional and digital media is Oreo's "Dunk in the Dark" tweet during the 2013 Super Bowl blackout. While Oreo had already invested in a traditional TV commercial during the game, their real-time response to the unexpected event on Twitter showcased the power of agile, digital engagement. This clever use of social media not only capitalized on the broad audience attention from the traditional ad but also amplified the brand's message through timely, relatable content, demonstrating the synergistic potential of integrating traditional and digital media.

CHAPTER 12. DIGITAL MARKETING IN THE MODERN ERA

In the rapidly evolving landscape of the 21st century, digital marketing stands as a beacon of progress, innovation, and connection. "Digital Marketing in the Modern Era" embarks on a comprehensive exploration of this dynamic field, elucidating the core principles, strategies, and technologies that are shaping the way brands interact with consumers. From the foundational shift towards digital platforms to the sophisticated use of analytics and data, this chapter delves into the multifaceted aspects of digital marketing, offering readers a panoramic view of its current state and future potential.

At the heart of digital marketing is the recognition of the internet not just as a communication tool, but as a vibrant ecosystem where brands and consumers coexist in a continuous dialogue. The chapter highlights the transition from traditional marketing methods to digital tactics, emphasizing the importance of adaptability and strategic thinking in an online world. With the advent of social media, search engine optimization (SEO), and content marketing, the ways in which marketers can reach and engage their audiences have multiplied exponentially, offering unprecedented opportunities for personalized and impactful marketing efforts.

Moreover, the chapter addresses the challenges and ethical considerations inherent to digital marketing. It navigates through the complexities of data privacy, the responsibility of marketers in the digital age, and the need for transparency in online interactions. Through real-world examples and case studies, it showcases how leading brands have successfully navigated the digital landscape, employing innovative strategies to capture attention, foster loyalty, and drive growth.

"Digital Marketing in the Modern Era" also casts a forward-looking gaze, pondering the future of digital marketing amidst rapid technological advancements. It speculates on the role of emerging technologies such as artificial intelligence, virtual reality, and blockchain in shaping the next wave of marketing strategies. As the digital world continues to expand and evolve, the chapter encourages marketers to remain vigilant, creative, and informed, ready to embrace new tools and methodologies to stay ahead in the game.

In essence, this chapter serves as both a roadmap and a call to action for marketers aiming to harness the power of digital marketing. It underscores the transformative potential of digital strategies to not only reach consumers but to connect with them on a deeper level, creating meaningful experiences that resonate in the digital age.

12.1 HARNESSING ONLINE ADVERTISING AND SOCIAL MEDIA

In the digital era, the power and potential of online advertising and social media as integral components of marketing strategies are undeniable. These platforms offer unprecedented opportunities for brands to connect with their audience, leveraging the vast reach and precision targeting capabilities inherent to the digital domain. This section explores how businesses can harness online advertising and social media to enhance visibility, engage with customers, and drive conversions.

The Dynamics of Online Advertising

Online advertising encompasses a broad spectrum of formats, including search engine marketing (SEM), display ads, video ads, and sponsored content. Each format serves unique objectives, from building brand awareness to driving website traffic and sales.

Search Engine Marketing (SEM)

SEM, a critical component of online advertising, involves placing ads on search engine results pages (SERPs) to capture the attention of users actively searching for related information, products, or services. Google Ads and Bing Ads are prominent platforms offering SEM services, allowing advertisers to bid on keywords and pay only when their ads are clicked (pay-per-click, PPC). The effectiveness of SEM lies in its ability to target users with high purchase intent, making it an efficient tool for driving immediate traffic and conversions.

Display and Video Ads

Display ads appear on websites within an advertising network, targeting users based on their browsing behavior, interests, and demographics. Video ads, often hosted on platforms like YouTube, offer dynamic content that can engage users more deeply than static images or text. Both display and video ads play vital roles in creating visual impact and enhancing brand recall.

Leveraging Social Media

Social media platforms are powerful tools for building brand presence, engaging with customers, and amplifying content. Each platform caters to different demographics and interests, enabling brands to tailor their strategies accordingly.

Building Community and Engagement

Platforms like Facebook, Instagram, and Twitter allow brands to create a sense of community by engaging with their audience through posts, comments, and direct messages. This two-way communication fosters a stronger brand-customer relationship and enhances loyalty.

Influencer Collaborations

Collaborating with influencers who have established credibility and a loyal following on social media can significantly amplify a brand's reach and authenticity. Influencer partnerships enable brands to tap into new audiences and leverage the trust that influencers have built with their followers.

Paid Social Advertising

Paid social advertising involves creating sponsored content that appears on users' social media feeds. These ads can be highly targeted based on extensive demographic, geographic, and behavioral data available on social media platforms. The customizable nature of paid social ads makes them an effective tool for reaching specific audience segments with tailored messages.

Integrating Online Advertising and Social Media

The key to harnessing online advertising and social media lies in a strategic, integrated approach that aligns with the brand's overall marketing objectives. Successful integration involves:

Cross-Platform Consistency: Ensuring that messaging and visual identity are consistent across online ads and social media platforms to build a cohesive brand image.

Data-Driven Targeting: Utilizing data analytics to refine targeting strategies and optimize ad spend for better ROI.

Engaging Content: Crafting content that resonates with the audience, encourages interaction, and supports the brand's narrative.

Measuring and Adapting: Continuously monitoring campaign performance across platforms to gather insights and adjust strategies for improved outcomes.

12.2 CRAFTING EFFECTIVE EMAIL MARKETING AND CONTENT STRATEGIES

In the diverse ecosystem of digital marketing, email marketing and content strategies stand out for their ability to establish direct, meaningful connections with audiences. These methods not only help in nurturing leads and building customer loyalty but also play a pivotal role in educating and engaging users, thereby driving conversions and brand advocacy. This section explores the intricacies of developing effective email marketing campaigns and content strategies that resonate with and captivate the intended audience.

Email Marketing: Personalization and Precision

Email marketing, one of the oldest forms of digital communication, remains incredibly effective due to its direct approach and personalization capabilities. It allows brands to send targeted messages to specific segments of their audience, fostering a sense of individual attention and relevance.

Segmentation and Targeting

The first step to a successful email marketing campaign is segmenting the audience based on their behaviors, preferences, and past interactions with the brand. This segmentation enables the delivery of personalized content that speaks directly to the needs and interests of each group, increasing the likelihood of engagement and conversion.

Automation and Drip Campaigns

Automation tools have revolutionized email marketing by enabling the creation of drip campaigns—scheduled sequences of emails that guide subscribers through a predefined pathway, depending on their actions or the time elapsed since their last interaction. This method ensures timely and relevant communication, gently nudging the audience towards the desired action, whether it's making a purchase, signing up for a webinar, or simply staying engaged with the brand.

Measuring Success

The effectiveness of email marketing is measurable through metrics such as open rates, click-through rates (CTR), and conversion rates. These indicators help marketers refine their strategies, tailoring content, and timing to better meet the needs of their audience.

Content Strategies: Value and Engagement

Content marketing is a strategic approach focused on creating and distributing valuable, relevant, and consistent content to attract and retain a clearly defined audience — and, ultimately, to drive profitable customer action. It's about understanding the audience's needs and answering them with informative, entertaining, or inspiring content.

Diverse Formats

Effective content strategies employ a variety of formats, including blog posts, videos, infographics, podcasts, and more, to cater to different preferences and consumption habits. For instance, a comprehensive blog post can establish thought leadership, while an engaging video can boost social media engagement.

SEO Integration

Integrating search engine optimization (SEO) into content creation ensures that the material not only appeals to the target audience but also ranks well in search engine results, enhancing visibility and traffic. Keyword research, on-page optimization, and quality backlinking are essential components of SEO that help content reach its intended audience.

Consistency and Quality

The keys to successful content marketing are consistency and quality. Regularly publishing high-quality content helps build a loyal following, establishes brand authority, and improves online visibility. It's not just about quantity; the content must provide real value to the audience, addressing their questions, challenges, and interests.

Integrating Email and Content Strategies

Combining email marketing with a solid content strategy can create a powerful synergy, driving engagement and conversions. Email can serve as a distribution channel for content, bringing personalized recommendations and updates directly to the subscriber's inbox. Meanwhile, content can fuel email marketing campaigns with fresh, engaging material that keeps the audience informed and interested.

12.3 AI AND MACHINE LEARNING IN DIGITAL CAMPAIGNS

The integration of Artificial Intelligence (AI) and Machine Learning (ML) into digital marketing campaigns represents a seismic shift in how brands interact with their audiences. These technologies offer the ability to analyze vast amounts of data, predict user behavior, and automate complex processes, thereby enhancing personalization, efficiency, and effectiveness of marketing efforts. This section explores the pivotal role of AI and ML in transforming digital campaigns, from predictive analytics and personalization to chatbots and advanced customer segmentation.

Predictive Analytics: Anticipating Customer Needs

Predictive analytics utilizes AI and ML algorithms to analyze historical data and predict future behaviors, preferences, and purchase patterns of customers. This foresight allows marketers to anticipate market trends, identify potential customer segments, and tailor their strategies to meet the audience's future needs.

Example: E-commerce Recommendations

Online retailers like Amazon use predictive analytics to power their recommendation engines, suggesting products to users based on their browsing history, purchase behavior, and items liked or purchased by similar users. This level of personalization enhances the shopping experience, increases customer satisfaction, and boosts sales.

Personalization at Scale

AI and ML enable personalization at an unprecedented scale, allowing brands to deliver tailored messages, offers, and content to individual users based on their unique behaviors and preferences. This granular level of personalization was previously unattainable due to the sheer volume of data and the complexity of user interactions.

Example: Dynamic Email Content

Marketers can use AI to dynamically change the content of emails based on the recipient's past interactions with the brand. For instance, a travel company could send personalized email newsletters featuring destination recommendations and special offers tailored to each subscriber's travel preferences and booking history.

Chatbots and Virtual Assistants: Enhancing Customer Experience

Chatbots and virtual assistants, powered by AI, provide instant, 24/7 customer service across various digital platforms. These AI-driven tools can handle a wide range of tasks, from answering FAQs and guiding users through the purchase process to providing personalized product recommendations.

Example: Customer Support and Engagement

Many businesses deploy chatbots on their websites and social media platforms to engage visitors the moment they arrive, offering assistance, gathering feedback, and even conducting transactions. This immediate interaction improves the customer experience, boosts engagement, and can significantly increase conversion rates.

Advanced Customer Segmentation

AI and ML facilitate advanced customer segmentation by analyzing complex datasets to identify patterns, behaviors, and preferences that may not be apparent through traditional analysis methods. This enables marketers to create highly targeted campaigns that speak directly to the needs of specific audience segments.

Example: Behavioral Segmentation for Targeted Campaigns

By analyzing user interaction data across websites and social media, AI can help marketers segment their audience based on behavior (e.g., frequent buyers, cart abandoners) and engage them with customized messaging designed to drive specific actions, such as completing a purchase or re-engaging with the brand.

CHAPTER 13. FRONTIERS OF MOBILE MARKETING AND NEW TECHNOLOGIES

In the digital age, mobile marketing and emerging technologies are fundamentally reshaping the marketing landscape, creating unprecedented avenues for brands to engage with consumers in more personalized, immersive, and interactive ways. The widespread adoption of smartphones, alongside advancements in artificial intelligence (AI), virtual reality (VR), and other groundbreaking technologies, has catalyzed a seismic shift in marketing strategies. These developments empower brands to forge deeper, more meaningful connections with their audiences, transcending traditional engagement methods.

This chapter embarks on an exploratory journey through the dynamic and evolving realm of mobile marketing, examining how the integration of cutting-edge technologies is revolutionizing the way brands interact with consumers. It delves into how mobile platforms have become the epicenter of consumer engagement, offering marketers the tools to deliver content that is not only highly personalized but also contextually relevant and timely. The chapter further explores the synergistic potential of mobile marketing when combined with AI and VR, highlighting how these technologies enhance the customer experience, offering tailored, immersive experiences that captivate and delight.

Moreover, the chapter underscores the strategic importance of leveraging these technologies to stay ahead in a competitive landscape where consumer expectations are constantly evolving. It discusses the challenges and opportunities that come with integrating new technologies into marketing strategies, emphasizing the need for marketers to adopt a forward-thinking mindset and to continuously explore innovative ways to leverage mobile platforms and emerging technologies.

As we navigate through the frontiers of mobile marketing and new technologies, this chapter aims to equip marketers with the insights and strategies needed to harness the full potential of these digital tools. It sets the stage for a future where marketing is not just about reaching consumers but engaging them in an ongoing, interactive dialogue, facilitated by technology that's always at the cutting edge of innovation.

13.1 STRATEGIES FOR EFFECTIVE MOBILE MARKETING

In the rapidly evolving digital landscape, mobile marketing has emerged as a critical channel for reaching and engaging consumers. With the increasing prevalence of smartphones and tablets, mobile devices have become an integral part of people's daily lives, offering marketers unprecedented opportunities to connect with their audience anytime, anywhere. Effective mobile marketing strategies leverage the unique characteristics of mobile devices to deliver personalized, timely, and relevant content to users. This section explores key strategies for maximizing the impact of mobile marketing campaigns.

Optimizing for Mobile Devices

The foundation of effective mobile marketing is ensuring that all content and digital properties are optimized for mobile devices. This includes responsive website design, fast loading times, and easy navigation on smaller screens. Mobile optimization enhances the user experience, improves search engine rankings, and increases the likelihood of conversion.

Example: Responsive Web Design

A responsive website automatically adjusts its layout and content to fit the screen size of the device it's being viewed on, providing an optimal browsing experience for users whether they're on a smartphone, tablet, or desktop.

Utilizing SMS and MMS Marketing

SMS (Short Message Service) and MMS (Multimedia Messaging Service) marketing are powerful tools for direct communication with consumers. These channels allow brands to send text messages or multimedia content directly to users' mobile devices, making them ideal for time-sensitive offers, alerts, and personalized communication.

Example: Flash Sale Notifications

Retailers can use SMS marketing to alert subscribers about flash sales, providing a direct link to the sale page. This strategy can drive immediate traffic and sales by leveraging the immediacy and personal nature of text messaging.

Leveraging Mobile Apps

Mobile apps offer a unique platform for engaging with consumers, providing a more immersive and interactive experience than traditional websites. Brands can use apps to deliver personalized content, loyalty programs, and exclusive offers, enhancing customer engagement and loyalty.

Example: Loyalty Apps

Coffee shops and restaurants often develop their own mobile apps to manage loyalty programs, allowing customers to collect rewards, order ahead, and receive personalized offers based on their purchase history.

Implementing Location-Based Marketing

Location-based marketing utilizes GPS technology to target consumers based on their geographic location. This strategy can include geofencing, which sends notifications to users' mobile devices when they enter a specific area, and beacon technology, which offers more precise location targeting within smaller spaces like stores.

Example: Geofencing for Retail Promotions

A retail store can set up a geofence around its location to send special offers or coupons to customers' mobile devices when they are nearby, encouraging them to visit the store.

Incorporating Mobile Advertising

Mobile advertising encompasses a range of formats, from in-app ads and mobile search ads to social media ads optimized for mobile devices. These ads can be highly targeted based on user demographics, behavior, and location, increasing their effectiveness.

Example: In-App Advertising

Gaming apps often incorporate in-app advertising, offering users rewards for watching video ads. This strategy can increase ad engagement and provide value to both the user and the advertiser.

Enhancing Customer Experience with AR and VR

Augmented Reality (AR) and Virtual Reality (VR) technologies offer innovative ways to enhance the mobile user experience. Brands can use AR and VR for virtual try-ons, product demonstrations, and immersive experiences that engage users in a novel and memorable way.

Example: Virtual Try-Ons

Cosmetic brands can use AR technology to allow users to virtually try on makeup products using their mobile device's camera, helping customers make informed purchase decisions without visiting a store.

13.2 EXPLORING THE IMPACT OF AI AND VR ON MARKETING

The advent of Artificial Intelligence (AI) and Virtual Reality (VR) technologies has ushered in a new era for marketing, transforming how brands interact with their customers and offering unprecedented levels of personalization and immersive experiences. These technologies not only enhance the efficiency and effectiveness of marketing strategies but also redefine the boundaries of customer engagement and product visualization. This section delves into the profound impact of AI and VR on the marketing landscape, showcasing their potential to revolutionize brand storytelling, customer service, and user experience.

The Role of AI in Personalized Marketing

AI has become a cornerstone in the evolution of personalized marketing, enabling brands to analyze large volumes of data to gain insights into consumer behavior and preferences. This deep understanding allows for the delivery of highly targeted content, recommendations, and experiences to individual users, significantly increasing the relevance and effectiveness of marketing efforts.

Predictive Personalization

By leveraging predictive analytics, AI can forecast future consumer behavior, preferences, and purchasing decisions with remarkable accuracy. This enables marketers to tailor their messaging and offers to meet the anticipated needs of their audience, often before the consumers themselves are aware of these needs.

Chatbots and Conversational Marketing

AI-powered chatbots and virtual assistants have transformed customer service and engagement, providing 24/7 interaction points that can handle inquiries, resolve issues, and even conduct transactions. This constant availability and the ability to deliver instant, personalized responses improve customer satisfaction and loyalty.

VR's Impact on Immersive Marketing Experiences

VR offers a groundbreaking platform for immersive marketing, allowing brands to create virtual experiences that engage customers in ways previously impossible. From virtual tours and product demonstrations to fully immersive brand worlds, VR provides a unique medium for storytelling and product interaction.

Virtual Showrooms and Product Demonstrations

VR technology enables businesses to create virtual showrooms and product demonstrations, allowing customers to explore products in a three-dimensional, interactive environment. This is particularly valuable for industries like real estate, automotive, and retail, where the spatial and tactile experience of the product plays a crucial role in the purchasing decision.

Enhanced Training and Onboarding

VR also offers innovative solutions for employee training and customer onboarding, presenting complex information in an engaging and digestible format. By simulating real-life scenarios, VR can effectively train staff in customer service, sales techniques, and product knowledge, enhancing their performance and confidence.

Integrating AI and VR for Marketing Innovation

The combination of AI and VR technologies presents exciting opportunities for marketing innovation. AI can enhance VR experiences by personalizing them based on user behavior and preferences, creating dynamic, adaptive environments that respond to the user's actions and interests.

Example: Personalized Virtual Experiences

Imagine a virtual retail store that adapts its layout, product selection, and promotions in real-time based on the individual preferences and past behavior of the shopper, powered by AI analysis. This level of personalization can significantly enhance the shopping experience, making it more engaging, efficient, and satisfying for the customer.

CHAPTER 14. CROSSING BORDERS: GLOBAL MARKETING STRATEGIES

In an era where the digital and physical realms coalesce, the chapter on "Crossing Borders: Global Marketing Strategies" underscores the imperative for brands to navigate the complex tapestry of global markets with agility and insight. This chapter embarks on a journey through the multifaceted landscape of global marketing, unraveling the threads of cultural nuance, regulatory hurdles, and the strategic finesse required to resonate with diverse audiences worldwide.

At its core, the discourse pivots around the nuanced understanding that global marketing transcends mere geographical expansion. It delves into the art and science of tailoring brand messages, ensuring they not only reach but also deeply connect with individuals across varying cultural, linguistic, and economic spectrums. The chapter illuminates the intricacies of international market entry strategies, from direct exports to forming strategic alliances, each pathway offering its blend of opportunities and challenges, underscored by real-world examples that bring these concepts to life.

A significant emphasis is placed on the criticality of cultural intelligence in global marketing endeavors. The narrative weaves through the strategies for navigating the complex web of cross-cultural communication, underscoring the importance of cultural sensitivity, localization of marketing efforts, and the strategic use of local influencers to foster authenticity and enhance consumer engagement.

Moreover, the chapter addresses the contemporary challenges that brands face in the global arena, including digital transformation, consumer behavior shifts, and the need for agility in the face of rapid market and technological changes. It outlines strategic approaches for overcoming these hurdles, emphasizing the role of data analytics, customer-centricity, and the integration of digital platforms in crafting marketing strategies that are not only globally expansive but also locally resonant and culturally pertinent. This chapter serves as a comprehensive guide for marketers aiming to navigate the global marketing landscape. It offers a blend of strategic insights, practical advice, and visionary foresight, equipping readers with the tools and understanding necessary to embark on global marketing ventures that are not only successful but also culturally enriching and socially responsible.

14.1 APPROACHES TO INTERNATIONAL MARKET ENTRY

Navigating the complexities of international market entry is a critical step for companies looking to expand their footprint globally. The choice of entry strategy is influenced by factors such as market size, customer preferences, regulatory environment, and the company's long-term objectives. This section explores various approaches to international market entry, each offering distinct advantages and challenges.

Exporting

Exporting is often the initial mode of entry for companies venturing into new markets. It involves selling products or services produced in one country to customers in another, either directly to consumers or through intermediaries. This approach requires minimal investment and risk but offers limited control over marketing and sales processes.

Advantages: Low risk and investment; quick market entry.

Challenges: Dependence on local distributors; limited control over marketing and distribution.

Licensing and Franchising

Licensing allows a company in the target country to use the property of the licensor, such as patents, trademarks, or business methods, in exchange for a fee or royalty. Franchising extends this concept by allowing the franchisee to use the company's entire business model and brand.

Advantages: Low risk; capital not tied up in foreign operations; expanded brand presence.

Challenges: Loss of control over product quality and brand reputation; limited revenue potential compared to direct operations.

Joint Ventures and Strategic Alliances

Entering a joint venture involves partnering with a local company to form a new entity, sharing resources, risks, and profits. Strategic alliances, while not involving the creation of a new entity, also entail collaboration with local firms to achieve specific business objectives.

Advantages: Access to local market knowledge and networks; shared risks and costs; compliance with local ownership regulations.

Challenges: Potential for conflicts between partners; shared control can complicate decision-making.

Wholly Owned Subsidiaries

Establishing a wholly owned subsidiary means setting up a new operation or acquiring an existing business in the foreign market. This approach offers complete control over operations but involves significant investment and risk.

Advantages: Full control over operations; potential for larger profits; direct contact with customers.

Challenges: High financial and political risk; large initial investment; complex legal and regulatory compliance.

E-commerce and Digital Platforms

Leveraging online marketplaces or creating a direct-to-consumer e-commerce platform can be an effective way to enter international markets without the need for physical presence. This approach has gained popularity with the rise of digital technology.

Advantages: Access to global markets with lower investment; flexibility in testing markets and scaling operations.

Challenges: Intense global competition; logistical challenges; need for localized digital marketing strategies.

Choosing the Right Approach

The optimal approach to international market entry varies depending on the company's products or services, industry dynamics, and specific market conditions. Companies should conduct thorough market research, including legal, cultural, and economic assessments, to inform their entry strategy. Additionally, understanding local consumer behavior and preferences is crucial for tailoring offerings and marketing strategies to meet the needs of the target market.

Successful international expansion requires a blend of strategic planning, local market insight, and adaptability to navigate the complexities of global markets. By carefully selecting their mode of entry and committing to understanding and respecting local cultures and practices, companies can establish a strong international presence and drive long-term growth.

14.2 OVERCOMING CHALLENGES IN CROSS-CULTURAL MARKETING

Cross-cultural marketing is the strategic process of marketing among consumers whose culture differs from that of the company's own culture. This approach is essential for brands expanding internationally, as it involves navigating a myriad of cultural nuances that influence consumer behavior and preferences. Successfully overcoming the challenges of cross-cultural marketing is crucial for building brand loyalty, enhancing brand perception, and avoiding missteps that could lead to brand damage. This section explores strategies to effectively manage and leverage cultural differences in global marketing efforts.

Understanding Cultural Nuances

Key Strategy: Conduct in-depth cultural research to understand the values, beliefs, and behaviors of the target market. This involves going beyond surface-level observations to grasp the underlying cultural drivers that influence purchasing decisions.

Application: Use local market experts or cultural consultants to gain insights. Tools like Hofstede's Cultural Dimensions can also provide a framework for understanding cultural differences.

Localizing Marketing Messages

Key Strategy: Adapt marketing messages and campaigns to reflect local languages, idioms, and cultural references. Localization goes beyond translation, ensuring that content is relevant and resonates with local audiences.

Application: Develop marketing materials with local teams or agencies that understand the local context. Test content with focus groups to ensure it aligns with local expectations and cultural norms.

Building Cultural Sensitivity

Key Strategy: Foster an organizational culture of sensitivity and respect towards diverse cultures. Training teams on cultural awareness can prevent misinterpretations and offensive content.

Application: Implement regular training sessions on cultural competence for employees, especially those involved in international marketing and customer service.

Leveraging Local Influencers

Key Strategy: Collaborate with local influencers who embody the cultural values and preferences of the target market. Influencers can act as brand ambassadors, providing authenticity and credibility to marketing efforts.

Application: Identify and partner with influencers who have a strong connection with the local audience. Tailor collaborations to ensure they feel genuine and culturally appropriate.

Customizing Product Offerings

Key Strategy: Tailor products and services to meet the specific needs and preferences of local markets. This may involve modifications to existing products or the development of new offerings.

Application: Conduct market research to identify local consumer needs that are unmet by the current product lineup. Consider local tastes, traditions, and usage patterns in product development.

Navigating Legal and Ethical Considerations

Key Strategy: Understand and comply with local laws, regulations, and ethical standards related to marketing and advertising. This includes data protection laws, advertising standards, and consumer rights.

Application: Work closely with legal experts to ensure all marketing activities are compliant with local regulations. Implement ethical guidelines that respect local cultural and social norms.

14.3 CONTEMPORARY GLOBAL MARKETING CHALLENGES AND STRATEGIES

In today's rapidly evolving global marketplace, companies face a multitude of challenges as they strive to connect with diverse audiences across different regions. These challenges are not only rooted in navigating cultural differences but also in adapting to technological advancements, changing consumer behaviors, and the global economic landscape. This section outlines contemporary global marketing challenges and the strategies businesses can employ to navigate these complexities successfully.

Digital Transformation and Market Fragmentation

Challenge: The digital revolution has transformed consumer behavior, with more customers moving online for their shopping needs. Additionally, market fragmentation has increased, with niche markets and personalized consumer preferences becoming more prevalent.

Strategies:

Leverage Data Analytics: Utilize big data and analytics to understand consumer behaviors and preferences across different markets.

Agile Marketing: Adopt flexible and agile marketing strategies that can quickly adapt to changing consumer trends and technological advancements.

Cultural Sensitivity and Localization

Challenge: As brands expand globally, they must ensure that their marketing messages are culturally sensitive and appropriately localized to avoid offending local sensibilities.

Strategies:

Deep Cultural Research: Invest in comprehensive cultural research to gain insights into the local culture, traditions, and consumer behaviors.

Local Partnerships: Collaborate with local partners, influencers, and marketing agencies who have an intimate understanding of the local market.

Navigating Regulatory Environments

Challenge: Global companies must navigate a complex web of regulations and laws that vary significantly from one country to another, including advertising standards, data protection laws, and product regulations.

Strategies:

Legal Expertise: Engage with legal experts who specialize in international trade and marketing law to ensure compliance in each market.

Standardization vs. Adaptation: Balance the standardization of global marketing campaigns with the need for adaptation to meet local regulations and consumer expectations.

Balancing Global and Local Needs

Challenge: Finding the right balance between creating a consistent global brand identity and catering to local tastes and preferences can be challenging.

Strategies:

Glocalization: Implement a "glocal" strategy that combines global branding with local marketing tactics to resonate with local audiences.

Consumer-Centric Approach: Prioritize the needs and preferences of local consumers when adapting products, services, and marketing messages.

Technological Adoption and Innovation

Challenge: Keeping pace with rapid technological advancements and integrating new technologies into marketing strategies is essential for staying competitive.

Strategies:

Innovation Labs: Establish innovation labs or collaborate with tech startups to explore new marketing technologies and platforms.

Continuous Learning: Foster a culture of continuous learning and development within the organization to embrace new technologies and digital marketing tools.

Sustainable and Ethical Marketing

Challenge: Consumers are increasingly demanding transparency, sustainability, and ethical practices from brands, making it crucial for companies to integrate these values into their global marketing strategies.

Strategies:

Sustainability Reporting: Publicly report on sustainability efforts and achievements to build trust with global consumers.

Ethical Supply Chains: Ensure that supply chains are ethical and sustainable, reflecting the brand's commitment to social and environmental responsibility.

PART IV: MEASURING AND ENHANCING MARKETING PERFORMANCE

Airbnb's 'Belong Anywhere' Campaign

(AI Generated Photo)

Airbnb's "Belong Anywhere" campaign, launched in 2015, was a significant move to rebrand the company and connect more deeply with its users. The campaign was centered around the concept of belonging and featured real stories from Airbnb hosts and guests from around the world. These stories were shared in a series of compelling videos that were distributed across various digital platforms.

The campaign effectively communicated the idea that Airbnb offers more than just a place to stay; it offers the opportunity to live like a local and experience a sense of belonging anywhere in the world. This message resonated with audiences who were looking for more authentic and immersive travel experiences.

The success of the "Belong Anywhere" campaign was evident in its ability to evoke emotions, inspire travel, and position Airbnb as a leader in offering unique travel experiences. The campaign also demonstrated the power of storytelling and emotional connection in modern digital marketing, as well as the importance of understanding and tapping into the aspirations of the target audience.

CHAPTER 15. THE ROLE OF DATA IN MARKETING

In today's digital landscape, data stands as the bedrock upon which effective marketing strategies are built, offering brands an unparalleled lens through which to view, understand, and connect with their target audiences. This transformative power of data has not only recalibrated the way brands approach marketing but has also equipped them with the tools to make more informed decisions, personalize consumer experiences, and gauge the success of their marketing initiatives with a level of precision previously unattainable.

This chapter delves into the expansive role of data in shaping modern marketing practices. It underscores how data's ability to provide deep insights into consumer behavior and preferences has become a crucial element in crafting strategies that are both engaging and effective. Furthermore, it highlights the significance of data in evaluating the return on investment (ROI) of marketing activities, offering a clear picture of their impact and guiding brands on where to allocate resources for maximum effect.

As we navigate through the realms of big data and analytics, the chapter sheds light on emerging trends that are defining the future of marketing. From predictive analytics that forecast consumer behavior to real-time data processing that allows for instant strategic adjustments, the text explores how these advancements are enabling marketers to stay ahead in an ever-evolving digital environment.

Moreover, the ethical considerations surrounding data usage are brought to the forefront, emphasizing the importance of navigating the fine line between leveraging data for marketing success and respecting consumer privacy. This discussion invites readers to consider the implications of data-driven marketing practices, advocating for a balanced approach that values ethical standards and builds trust with consumers.

Through its comprehensive exploration of the role of data in marketing, this chapter provides readers with a thorough understanding of how data's integral role in modern marketing strategies is not only enhancing the way brands interact with their audiences but also setting new benchmarks for transparency, efficiency, and personalization in the digital age.

15.1 LEVERAGING MARKETING ANALYTICS FOR INSIGHT

In the contemporary marketing landscape, leveraging analytics for insight has become a cornerstone for businesses aiming to navigate the complexities of consumer behavior and competitive environments. Marketing analytics offers a detailed view of performance across various channels, enabling marketers to make data-driven decisions that enhance campaign effectiveness, optimize budget allocation, and tailor consumer experiences. This section explores the strategic utilization of marketing analytics to gain profound insights into marketing initiatives.

Understanding Marketing Analytics

Marketing analytics encompasses the processes and technologies that enable marketers to evaluate the success of their marketing initiatives by measuring performance (e.g., blogging versus social media versus channel communications) and understanding the effectiveness of their marketing strategies. This involves collecting data from across all marketing channels and consolidating it into a unified view that offers actionable insights and data-driven decision-making capabilities.

Key Components of Marketing Analytics

Data Collection and Management: The first step involves gathering data from various sources, including websites, social media, email campaigns, and digital ads. Effective data management practices ensure that this data is accurate, organized, and accessible.

Metrics and KPIs: Identifying the right metrics and key performance indicators (KPIs) is crucial for measuring success. Common KPIs include conversion rates, click-through rates, bounce rates, and customer acquisition costs. These metrics provide a quantitative basis for evaluating marketing strategies.

Analytical Tools and Software: Utilizing advanced analytical tools and software enables marketers to sift through data and extract meaningful insights. Platforms like Google Analytics, Adobe Analytics, and specialized marketing automation tools offer comprehensive analytics capabilities, including user behavior analysis, campaign performance tracking, and predictive analytics.

Customer Segmentation: Analytics allows marketers to segment their audience based on various criteria, such as demographics, behavior, and purchase history. This segmentation enables more targeted and personalized marketing efforts, improving engagement and conversion rates.

Predictive Analytics: By employing predictive models, marketers can forecast future trends, customer behaviors, and potential market changes. This foresight aids in proactive strategy planning and optimization.

Performance Optimization: Continuous analysis of marketing data helps identify what is working and what is not. Marketers can then fine-tune their strategies, reallocating resources to high-performing channels and tactics, and experimenting with new approaches for underperforming areas.

Implementing Insights for Strategic Decision-Making

The insights gained from marketing analytics should inform strategic decisions, guiding the development of more effective marketing campaigns. This involves:

Tailoring Content and Offers: Customize marketing messages and offers based on insights into customer preferences and behaviors.

Optimizing User Experience: Enhance the online user experience by understanding how users interact with websites and digital content.

Cross-channel Marketing Coordination: Ensure that insights inform a cohesive marketing strategy across all channels, providing a consistent and unified brand experience.

Budget Allocation: Allocate marketing budgets more efficiently by investing in channels and strategies that offer the highest ROI.

Challenges and Considerations

While marketing analytics offers numerous benefits, challenges such as data privacy concerns, the integration of data from disparate sources, and the need for skilled analysts to interpret complex data sets must be addressed.

Additionally, maintaining a balance between data-driven decision-making and creative marketing strategies is essential for holistic marketing success.

15.2 EVALUATING MARKETING ROI

Evaluating the Return on Investment (ROI) of marketing activities is pivotal for understanding their financial impact and guiding future marketing investments. It allows businesses to discern which strategies are generating value and how to allocate resources for maximum effectiveness. This section delves into the methodologies for assessing marketing ROI, highlighting key considerations and strategies for optimization.

Defining Marketing ROI

Marketing ROI is a performance measure used to evaluate the efficiency of an investment in marketing activities. It compares the profit generated from these activities against their cost, providing a clear picture of their contribution to the bottom line. Calculating ROI helps businesses justify marketing expenditures, identify successful tactics, and make informed decisions about future marketing strategies.

Calculating Marketing ROI

The basic formula for calculating marketing ROI is:

$$\text{ROI} = \left(\frac{\text{Net Profit from Marketing Efforts} - \text{Cost of Marketing Efforts}}{\text{Cost of Marketing Efforts}} \right) \times 100$$

Net Profit from Marketing Efforts: The revenue generated from marketing activities, minus the cost of goods sold (COGS) and other expenses directly related to producing the goods or services sold.

Cost of Marketing Efforts: The total expenses associated with executing the marketing campaigns, including advertising costs, salaries of marketing personnel, and other related expenses.

Key Considerations in Evaluating Marketing ROI

Attribution Models: Determining the most accurate way to attribute sales to specific marketing activities can be challenging. Different attribution models (e.g., last-click, first-click, multi-touch) can significantly affect ROI calculations.

Time Frame: The time frame considered for evaluating ROI can impact the results. Some marketing efforts, especially those aimed at building brand awareness or loyalty, may take longer to yield financial returns.

Non-Financial Metrics: While ROI focuses on financial returns, it's also essential to consider non-financial metrics such as customer engagement, brand awareness, and customer satisfaction, which can indirectly influence long-term profitability.

Strategies for Optimizing Marketing ROI

Data-Driven Decision Making: Utilize analytics and data to guide marketing decisions, focusing on strategies that have proven effective according to past ROI analyses.

Continuous Testing and Learning: Employ A/B testing and other experimental approaches to continually refine marketing tactics and strategies, optimizing for those that deliver the best ROI.

Integrated Marketing Approach: Ensure a cohesive marketing strategy across all channels, leveraging insights from each to inform a comprehensive approach that maximizes overall ROI.

Customer Lifetime Value (CLV) Consideration: Factor in the CLV when evaluating ROI to get a more holistic view of the profitability of marketing efforts, recognizing that acquiring a new customer can lead to repeated sales over time.

Efficiency in Spend: Regularly review and adjust marketing budgets based on performance data, reallocating resources to high-performing channels and cutting back on underperforming initiatives.

Challenges in Measuring Marketing ROI

Data Collection and Quality: Ensuring accurate and comprehensive data collection can be difficult, impacting the reliability of ROI calculations.

Changing Consumer Behavior: Rapid shifts in consumer behavior and market conditions can make it challenging to predict ROI accurately.

Digital Complexity: With the proliferation of digital marketing channels, attributing sales accurately across multiple touchpoints adds complexity to ROI evaluations.

15.3 TRENDS IN BIG DATA ANALYTICS

Big data analytics has become a critical component of strategic decision-making in marketing, offering insights that drive innovation, customer engagement, and competitive advantage. As technology advances, new trends emerge that redefine how businesses leverage big data to enhance their marketing strategies. This section explores the current trends in big data analytics and their implications for marketing.

Real-Time Data Analysis

Overview: The ability to analyze data in real-time is revolutionizing marketing strategies, enabling businesses to respond to customer behaviors and market changes instantaneously. Real-time analytics facilitates dynamic pricing, personalized marketing messages, and immediate customer service resolutions.

Impact: Marketers can now make data-driven decisions faster than ever, optimizing campaigns on the fly and enhancing customer experiences with timely interactions.

Predictive Analytics and Machine Learning

Overview: Predictive analytics, powered by machine learning algorithms, allows marketers to forecast future consumer behaviors, preferences, and trends. By analyzing historical and current data, businesses can predict outcomes with a high degree of accuracy, from customer churn rates to potential sales spikes.

Impact: This trend enables proactive marketing strategies, allowing businesses to anticipate customer needs, optimize inventory levels, and tailor marketing messages before the demand arises.

Customer Data Platforms (CDPs)

Overview: Customer Data Platforms (CDPs) are becoming essential for managing and integrating customer data across various sources and touchpoints. CDPs provide a unified customer database accessible by other systems, enabling a coherent, 360-degree view of the customer.

Impact: With CDPs, marketers can achieve a deeper understanding of their audience, facilitating personalized marketing campaigns and improving customer journey mapping.

Enhanced Data Visualization Tools

Overview: As big data becomes more complex, the importance of advanced data visualization tools grows. These tools transform large datasets into comprehensible, visual formats, making it easier for marketers to identify patterns, correlations, and insights.

Impact: Enhanced visualization aids in communicating complex data insights across the organization, supporting more informed decision-making and strategic planning.

Privacy-First Analytics

Overview: With increasing concerns over data privacy and the implementation of regulations like GDPR and CCPA, there's a growing trend towards privacy-first analytics. This approach prioritizes data protection and ethical data usage, ensuring compliance and building customer trust.

Impact: Marketers must adapt to these privacy constraints by developing strategies that respect consumer privacy while still deriving valuable insights from data analytics.

Integration of IoT Data

Overview: The Internet of Things (IoT) generates vast amounts of data from connected devices, offering unique insights into consumer behavior and preferences. Integrating IoT data into marketing analytics opens new avenues for personalized and context-aware marketing.

Impact: IoT integration allows marketers to understand how products are used in real life, enabling targeted marketing efforts based on actual usage patterns and environmental factors.

AI-Driven Content Creation

Overview: Artificial Intelligence (AI) is increasingly being used to generate content, from personalized email messages to product descriptions and advertising copy. This trend leverages data analytics to produce content that resonates with target audiences.

Impact: AI-driven content creation can significantly enhance content relevance and engagement, driving higher conversion rates and customer satisfaction.

15.4 ETHICS AND PRIVACY IN DATA-DRIVEN MARKETING

In the era of data-driven marketing, the collection and use of consumer data have become central to developing effective marketing strategies. However, this reliance on data raises significant ethical considerations and privacy concerns. As businesses navigate the complex landscape of digital marketing, they must balance the pursuit of insight with respect for individual privacy rights. This section explores the ethical challenges in data-driven marketing and outlines best practices for maintaining consumer trust and compliance with privacy regulations.

Ethical Challenges in Data Collection and Use

Transparency and Consent: Consumers often are unaware of the extent to which their data is collected, shared, and used for marketing purposes. Ensuring transparency and obtaining explicit consent for data collection and usage are fundamental ethical practices that respect consumer autonomy.

Data Minimization and Purpose Limitation: Collecting more data than necessary or using data for purposes other than those for which it was collected can breach consumer trust and privacy. Marketers should adhere to the principles of data minimization and purpose limitation, collecting only the data needed for specified, legitimate marketing activities.

Bias and Discrimination: Data-driven marketing algorithms can inadvertently perpetuate biases or lead to discriminatory practices, such as excluding certain demographics from marketing campaigns or credit offers. Marketers must be vigilant in identifying and mitigating algorithmic biases to ensure fairness and inclusivity.

Navigating Privacy Regulations

Global Data Protection Regulations: With the introduction of regulations like the General Data Protection Regulation (GDPR) in Europe and the California Consumer Privacy Act (CCPA) in the United States, businesses are required to adhere to strict guidelines regarding data privacy and consumer rights. Compliance with these and other regional privacy laws is essential for legal and ethical marketing practices.

Data Security: Protecting collected data against unauthorized access, breaches, and theft is a critical component of ethical data-driven marketing. Implementing robust data security measures, such as encryption and access controls, safeguards consumer information and maintains trust.

Best Practices for Ethical Data-Driven Marketing

Develop Clear Privacy Policies: Create transparent, easily understandable privacy policies that detail how consumer data is collected, used, and protected. Ensure these policies are accessible and communicate any changes to consumers promptly.

Implement Privacy by Design: Integrate privacy considerations into the development and implementation of marketing strategies from the outset. This approach ensures that privacy is a foundational element of data-driven marketing efforts.

Offer Opt-Out Options: Provide consumers with clear, simple mechanisms to opt-out of data collection and marketing communications. Respecting consumer choices is crucial for maintaining trust and ethical relationships.

Regularly Review Data Practices: Conduct regular audits of data collection, storage, and processing practices to ensure compliance with privacy regulations and ethical standards. This includes reviewing partnerships with third parties to ensure they also adhere to these standards.

Educate and Train Staff: Ensure that all employees, especially those involved in marketing and data management, are educated about the importance of data privacy and know how to comply with ethical and legal standards.

CHAPTER 16. CUSTOMER RELATIONSHIP MANAGEMENT (CRM)

In today's hyper-competitive business landscape, where customer loyalty is as elusive as it is valuable, Customer Relationship Management (CRM) emerges as a beacon of strategy for nurturing long-term customer relationships. CRM represents a paradigm shift from transactional marketing to a more relational approach, focusing on understanding and responding to individual customer needs over the entirety of their lifecycle. This chapter delves deep into the strategic importance of CRM, exploring how leveraging CRM systems and technologies can significantly enhance customer engagement, loyalty, and organizational profitability.

CRM systems serve as the technological backbone, providing an integrated platform to collect, analyze, and act on customer data across every touchpoint. This enables businesses to offer personalized experiences, anticipate customer needs, and resolve issues promptly, thereby fostering a sense of trust and loyalty. The strategic deployment of CRM goes beyond mere technology adoption; it encompasses a holistic approach to redefining customer interactions, aligning product and service offerings with customer expectations, and embedding customer-centricity into the organizational culture.

Key strategies for building lasting customer relationships are highlighted, focusing on personalization, consistent and meaningful communication, feedback loops, and exceptional customer service. These strategies underscore the importance of treating customers as unique individuals with distinct preferences and needs, facilitated by the rich insights derived from CRM data analytics.

The chapter further explores the use of CRM technologies to automate marketing and sales processes, enhance customer service, facilitate personalized communications, and gain insights through analytics. These functionalities underscore CRM's role in not just managing customer relationships but actively enhancing them through strategic engagement and interaction.

Additionally, this chapter addresses contemporary challenges in CRM, such as navigating the complexities of digital transformation, ensuring data privacy, and integrating CRM with other technological innovations. It underscores the evolving nature of CRM strategies in response to shifting consumer behaviors and technological advancements, emphasizing the need for businesses to remain agile and customer-focused in their CRM initiatives.

In essence, Customer Relationship Management is presented as a strategic imperative for businesses seeking to thrive in the modern marketplace. By effectively leveraging CRM systems and strategies, organizations can cultivate deeper, more meaningful relationships with their customers, driving sustained engagement, loyalty, and growth.

16.1 STRATEGIES FOR BUILDING LASTING CUSTOMER RELATIONSHIPS

Building lasting customer relationships is essential for sustained business success. It involves creating positive experiences that foster loyalty, trust, and a deep connection between the customer and the brand. In the age of Customer Relationship Management (CRM) systems, businesses have powerful tools at their disposal to personalize interactions, understand customer needs, and deliver exceptional service. Here are key strategies for nurturing enduring customer relationships.

Personalization at Scale

Overview: Tailoring experiences to individual customer preferences and behaviors to make interactions more relevant and engaging.

Application: Utilize CRM data to segment customers based on their purchase history, preferences, and behaviors. Craft personalized marketing messages, product recommendations, and offers that resonate with each segment or individual.

Consistent and Meaningful Communication

Overview: Maintaining regular contact with customers through their preferred channels to keep the brand top-of-mind and strengthen relationships.

Application: Develop a communication calendar that schedules regular touchpoints with customers, including newsletters, product updates, and personalized check-ins. Use CRM insights to determine the most effective communication channels for different customer segments.

Feedback Loops and Active Listening

Overview: Encouraging and acting on customer feedback to improve products, services, and experiences.

Application: Implement mechanisms for collecting customer feedback, such as surveys, feedback forms, and social media monitoring. Use CRM to track feedback trends and respond directly to customer concerns, demonstrating that their input is valued and acted upon.

Exceptional Customer Service

Overview: Providing prompt, efficient, and empathetic service to address customer inquiries and resolve issues.

Application: Leverage CRM tools to manage customer service inquiries, ensuring quick response times and personalized support based on the customer's history and profile. Train customer service teams to use CRM data to enhance the service experience.

Loyalty and Reward Programs

Overview: Rewarding repeat customers for their loyalty to encourage continued engagement and advocacy.

Application: Design a loyalty program that offers tangible benefits, such as discounts, exclusive access, or rewards points. Use CRM to track customer participation in the program and tailor rewards to their preferences and purchasing behavior.

Education and Value-Added Content

Overview: Offering educational content and resources that help customers get the most out of your products or services.

Application: Develop tutorials, guides, webinars, and blogs that address common questions and challenges. Use CRM data to personalize content recommendations based on the customer's interests and past interactions.

Community Building

Overview: Creating a sense of community among customers through shared experiences, values, or interests.

Application: Facilitate forums, social media groups, or events where customers can connect with each other and the brand. Use CRM insights to identify common interests among customers and foster a sense of belonging.

16.2 UTILIZING CRM SYSTEMS AND TECHNOLOGIES

Customer Relationship Management (CRM) systems and technologies play a pivotal role in modern business strategies, enabling organizations to streamline operations, enhance customer interactions, and drive sales. These tools offer a centralized platform for managing all aspects of customer engagement, from sales and marketing to customer service and analytics. This section explores effective ways to utilize CRM systems and technologies to bolster customer relationships and achieve business objectives.

Centralizing Customer Data

Overview: A unified customer database is the heart of any CRM system, providing a comprehensive view of customer interactions, preferences, and history across all touchpoints.

Application: Consolidate data from various sources, including sales transactions, customer service interactions, social media activity, and website visits, into the CRM system.

Ensure data accuracy and consistency to enable effective segmentation, personalized marketing, and targeted sales efforts.

Automating Marketing and Sales Processes

Overview: CRM technologies automate repetitive tasks, freeing up time for strategic activities and personal customer engagement.

Application: Implement automated email marketing campaigns that trigger based on specific customer actions or milestones.

Use CRM to automate lead scoring and assignment, ensuring that sales teams focus their efforts on the most promising prospects.

Enhancing Customer Service

Overview: CRM systems improve customer service efficiency and effectiveness by providing service representatives with immediate access to customer information and history.

Application: Equip customer service teams with CRM tools to quickly retrieve customer profiles, past interactions, and purchase history during support calls or chats.

Automate service ticket tracking and follow-up reminders to ensure timely resolution of customer issues.

Facilitating Personalized Communications

Overview: Personalization enhances customer engagement by delivering relevant and timely messages that resonate with individual preferences and needs.

Application: Leverage CRM data to segment customers based on behavior, demographics, and purchase history.

Tailor marketing messages, product recommendations, and special offers to individual customer segments.

Gaining Insights Through Analytics

Overview: CRM analytics transform data into actionable insights, helping businesses understand customer behavior, measure marketing effectiveness, and predict future trends.

Application: Utilize CRM dashboards and reporting tools to monitor key performance indicators (KPIs), such as customer lifetime value, conversion rates, and customer satisfaction scores.

Conduct cohort analysis to identify trends and patterns in customer behavior over time.

Integrating with Other Systems

Overview: CRM integration with other business systems and platforms ensures seamless data flow and enhances operational efficiency.

Application: Connect CRM systems with email platforms, social media management tools, e-commerce systems, and ERP software to enable a unified approach to customer management.

Use APIs or built-in integration capabilities to ensure real-time data synchronization across systems.

Mobile CRM Access

Overview: Mobile CRM solutions provide sales and service teams with access to customer data and CRM functionalities on the go.

Application: Deploy mobile CRM apps that allow sales representatives to update customer records, schedule meetings, and access sales materials from anywhere.

Enable service teams to use mobile CRM for on-site customer support, accessing service histories and documentation in real-time.

CHAPTER 17. ADDRESSING CONTEMPORARY MARKETING CHALLENGES

This chapter delves into the complexities faced by modern marketers amidst a landscape transformed by digital innovation, evolving consumer preferences, and intense global competition. This chapter emphasizes the necessity for agility, creativity, and a profound grasp of the digital domain to successfully navigate the shifting paradigms of consumer engagement, market expansion, and technological disruptions.

The narrative begins by exploring the dynamics of digital transformation, emphasizing its dual role as a catalyst for innovation and a source of formidable challenges. The focus is on adopting a customer-centric approach, integrating cutting-edge digital technologies, and fostering a culture of continuous learning and adaptability. This ensures organizations not only survive but thrive in an environment characterized by rapid change.

Subsequent discussions pivot to adapting to the ever-evolving consumer preferences, highlighting the importance of continuous market research, personalization, and customization in marketing strategies. The chapter illustrates how leveraging digital and social media platforms, emphasizing sustainability, and maintaining flexibility are crucial strategies for staying aligned with consumer expectations.

A significant portion of the narrative is dedicated to overcoming global marketing and technological disruptions. It outlines strategies for navigating cultural and regulatory diversity, overcoming language barriers, and adapting to varying degrees of digital transformation across markets. This includes leveraging global e-commerce platforms and managing tech disruptions to maintain a competitive edge and foster global brand presence. The chapter concludes by addressing the dual challenge of leveraging technology to enhance consumer experiences while ensuring data privacy and security. It advocates for a balanced approach that respects consumer privacy rights while harnessing the power of digital innovation to create meaningful, personalized customer interactions.

In essence, Addressing Contemporary Marketing Challenges serves as a comprehensive guide for marketers seeking to navigate the intricacies of the modern marketing landscape, offering strategies for leveraging digital transformation, adapting to consumer preferences, and overcoming global marketing and technological disruptions to achieve sustained success.

17.1 AVIGATING THE CHALLENGES OF DIGITAL TRANSFORMATION

Digital transformation represents a profound shift in the way businesses operate and engage with customers, driven by the rapid adoption of digital technologies. While offering significant opportunities for innovation and growth, this transformation also poses numerous challenges, from integrating new technologies to adapting to the digital consumer landscape. This section outlines strategies for effectively navigating the challenges of digital transformation in marketing.

Embracing a Customer-Centric Approach

Overview: At the heart of digital transformation is the need to put the customer at the center of all business and marketing strategies. This means understanding and meeting the evolving expectations of digital consumers.

Strategies:

Customer Insights: Leverage data analytics and customer feedback to gain deep insights into customer behavior, preferences, and pain points.

Personalization: Use these insights to deliver personalized experiences across all digital touchpoints, from websites and apps to social media and email marketing.

Integrating Digital Technologies

Overview: The integration of digital technologies into marketing strategies is essential for engaging today's tech-savvy consumers and optimizing operational efficiency.

Strategies:

Martech Stack Optimization: Carefully select and integrate marketing technology tools that align with your business goals and enhance customer engagement.

Cross-functional Collaboration: Foster collaboration between marketing, IT, and other departments to ensure a seamless integration of technologies across the business.

Cultivating Digital Skills and Mindset

Overview: The digital transformation requires not only new technologies but also new skill sets and a digital-first mindset among employees.

Strategies:

Training and Development: Invest in ongoing training and professional development programs to equip your team with the necessary digital marketing skills.

Cultural Change: Promote a culture of innovation, agility, and openness to change, encouraging employees to experiment with new ideas and technologies.

Adapting to the Pace of Change

Overview: The digital landscape is characterized by rapid and continuous change, requiring businesses to remain agile and responsive to keep up.

Strategies:

Agile Marketing: Adopt agile marketing practices that allow for flexibility, quick decision-making, and the ability to pivot strategies based on real-time data and market trends.

Innovation and Experimentation: Encourage a culture of innovation where experimenting with new digital tools, platforms, and strategies is supported and rewarded.

Ensuring Data Privacy and Security

Overview: With increased reliance on digital technologies and data comes the responsibility to protect consumer privacy and ensure data security.

Strategies:

Compliance with Regulations: Stay informed about and comply with data protection regulations such as GDPR and CCPA.

Data Security Measures: Implement robust cybersecurity measures to protect customer data from breaches and unauthorized access.

17.2 ADAPTING TO EVOLVING CONSUMER PREFERENCES

In today's rapidly changing marketplace, one of the most significant challenges marketers face is keeping pace with evolving consumer preferences. These shifts are influenced by a variety of factors, including technological advancements, social and environmental concerns, and cultural trends. Successfully adapting to these changes is crucial for businesses aiming to remain relevant and competitive. This section explores strategies for effectively responding to and anticipating changes in consumer behavior.

Continuous Market Research

Overview: Staying informed about current and emerging consumer trends is foundational to adapting marketing strategies effectively.

Strategies:

Utilize a Mix of Research Tools: Employ surveys, focus groups, social media listening, and analytics tools to gather comprehensive insights into consumer preferences.

Predictive Analytics: Leverage predictive analytics to forecast future trends and prepare marketing strategies that align with anticipated consumer behaviors.

Personalization and Customization

Overview: Personalized marketing approaches resonate more deeply with consumers, reflecting their desire for experiences and products that feel tailor-made.

Strategies:

Data-Driven Personalization: Use CRM and analytics platforms to tailor marketing messages, product recommendations, and customer experiences based on individual consumer data.

Segmentation: Segment your audience based on demographic, psychographic, and behavioral data to create more targeted and relevant marketing campaigns.

Embracing Digital and Social Media Platforms

Overview: Digital and social media platforms are pivotal in connecting with consumers, particularly younger demographics who spend a significant amount of time online.

Strategies:

Omnichannel Presence: Establish a strong brand presence across multiple digital platforms to engage consumers where they spend their time.

Interactive and Engaging Content: Create content that encourages interaction and engagement, such as live streams, polls, and user-generated content campaigns.

Sustainability and Ethical Marketing

Overview: Increasingly, consumers prefer brands that demonstrate a commitment to sustainability, ethical practices, and social responsibility.

Strategies:

Communicate Your Values: Clearly articulate your brand's commitment to sustainability and ethical practices in your marketing messages.

Authentic Initiatives: Implement genuine sustainability initiatives and social responsibility programs, avoiding superficial claims that could be perceived as greenwashing.

Flexibility and Agility

Overview: The ability to quickly adapt marketing strategies in response to shifting consumer preferences is a competitive advantage.

Strategies:

Agile Marketing Approaches: Adopt agile methodologies in your marketing processes, allowing for rapid iteration and responsiveness to market changes.

Continuous Optimization: Regularly review campaign performance and consumer feedback to optimize strategies in real time.

Leveraging Technology for Enhanced Experiences

Overview: Technological innovations offer new opportunities to create unique and immersive consumer experiences.

Strategies:

Augmented Reality (AR) and Virtual Reality (VR): Utilize AR and VR technologies to offer immersive product experiences or virtual try-ons.

AI and Machine Learning: Implement AI-driven chatbots for personalized customer service and machine learning algorithms for predictive product recommendations.

17.3 GLOBAL MARKETING CHALLENGES AND TECH DISRUPTIONS

Navigating the global marketplace presents unique challenges for businesses aiming to expand their reach across diverse cultures and economies. These challenges are compounded by rapid technological disruptions that continually reshape consumer behaviors and marketing landscapes. This section outlines strategies to address global marketing challenges and leverage technological advancements to maintain a competitive edge.

Addressing Cultural and Regulatory Diversity

Overview: Success in global marketing requires an understanding and respect for cultural nuances and adherence to varying regulatory environments.

Strategies:

Localized Marketing Strategies: Develop marketing campaigns that are not only translated but fully localized to reflect cultural sensitivities, preferences, and norms.

Regulatory Compliance: Stay informed about and ensure compliance with local laws and regulations, including data protection, advertising standards, and consumer rights.

Overcoming Language Barriers

Overview: Effective communication across multiple languages is a fundamental aspect of global marketing.

Strategies:

Professional Translation and Localization Services: Invest in high-quality translation services and work with local experts to ensure marketing materials are culturally and contextually appropriate.

Multilingual Customer Support: Provide customer service in the local languages of your target markets to enhance customer experiences and satisfaction.

Adapting to Digital Transformation

Overview: Digital transformation affects global markets differently, influenced by local technological infrastructure, internet penetration, and digital literacy.

Strategies:

Market-Specific Digital Strategies: Tailor digital marketing strategies to fit the technological landscape of each target market, considering the prevalence of mobile devices, social media platforms, and e-commerce adoption.

Innovative Digital Solutions: Leverage emerging technologies like AI, AR, and IoT to create differentiated and engaging customer experiences that cater to local market expectations.

Leveraging Global E-Commerce Platforms

Overview: E-commerce platforms offer a pathway to global markets, but competition is fierce, and consumer expectations are high.

Strategies:

Optimized Online Presence: Ensure your e-commerce site is optimized for international audiences, including currency conversion, global shipping options, and localized content.

Marketplace Integration: Consider selling on established global e-commerce marketplaces to capitalize on their reach and infrastructure while navigating the complexities of cross-border e-commerce.

Managing Tech Disruptions

Overview: Technological disruptions can render traditional marketing strategies obsolete, requiring businesses to continuously innovate and adapt.

Strategies:

Continuous Innovation: Foster a culture of innovation within your organization that encourages experimentation with new technologies and marketing tactics.

Agile Response to Market Changes: Develop agile marketing teams that can quickly respond to technological advancements and shifts in consumer behavior, ensuring your marketing strategies remain relevant and effective.

Building Resilient Supply Chains

Overview: Global marketing efforts can be undermined by disruptions in supply chains, highlighting the need for resilience and flexibility.

Strategies:

Diversification of Suppliers: Avoid over-reliance on single markets or suppliers by diversifying your supply chain geographically.

Technology-Enabled Supply Chains: Implement supply chain management technologies that provide real-time visibility and analytics, enabling proactive management of disruptions.

PART V: THE EVOLVING LANDSCAPE OF MARKETING

Guinness's 'Made of More' Campaign

(AI Generated Photo)

Guinness's "Made of More" campaign is a prime example of storytelling in marketing. One of the notable ads in this campaign was the story of the Liberty Fields RFC, a pioneering Japanese women's rugby team. Launched in conjunction with the 2019 Rugby World Cup held in Japan, the campaign featured a TV ad and a five-minute documentary.

The ad and documentary highlighted the challenges the team faced, including gender stereotypes and societal expectations in 1989 Tokyo. Despite these challenges, the team members defied social conventions and represented their country at the Women's World Cup. The story underscored the resilience, determination, and camaraderie of the team.

This campaign by Guinness was applauded for its authentic storytelling and emotional resonance. It connected with audiences by showcasing real people overcoming real challenges, aligning perfectly with Guinness's brand identity of resilience and character.

The campaign demonstrated how brands could effectively use storytelling to create a strong emotional connection with their audience and reinforce their brand values.

CHAPTER 18. EMERGING TRENDS AND FUTURE DIRECTIONS

This chapter embarks on a visionary journey into the ever-evolving realm of marketing. It acknowledges that the marketing landscape is subject to constant flux, driven by rapid technological advancements, shifting consumer preferences, and an increasing focus on sustainable and ethical business practices. This chapter serves as a forward-looking exploration, shedding light on the pivotal trends poised to reshape marketing strategies and the tools employed by marketers to forge meaningful connections with their global audiences.

The narrative begins by underscoring the influence of technological innovation on marketing. From artificial intelligence and machine learning to augmented reality and blockchain, these technologies offer unprecedented opportunities for personalized and immersive customer experiences. The chapter examines how these advancements enable marketers to understand and engage with consumers in more profound and nuanced ways.

Consumer expectations are another focal point, with today's consumers demanding more than just quality products and services. They seek authenticity, personalization, and brands that align with their values, particularly regarding sustainability and social responsibility. This section delves into how marketers can adapt to these expectations, crafting brand messages and experiences that resonate deeply with consumer values and aspirations.

Sustainability and ethical practices have transitioned from optional to imperative in the marketing playbook. The chapter discusses the growing importance of green marketing, ethical advertising, and corporate social responsibility, highlighting how these practices not only contribute to a better world but also foster long-term brand loyalty and trust.

Finally, the chapter ventures into speculative territory, exploring potential future directions of marketing. It considers the impact of emerging technologies not yet mainstream and anticipates how ongoing social and economic shifts could shape consumer behavior and marketing strategies in the years to come.

"Emerging Trends and Future Directions" is not just a chapter; it's a clarion call for marketers to remain agile, informed, and ethically grounded as they navigate the future. It encourages a proactive stance towards innovation, a deep commitment to understanding and meeting consumer needs, and a principled approach to contributing positively to society and the environment.

18.1 FORECASTING FUTURE TRENDS IN MARKETING

In the dynamic realm of marketing, staying ahead requires not just responding to current trends but anticipating future shifts. As we navigate through the digital age, several key trends are emerging, driven by technological advancements, changing consumer behaviors, and broader societal changes. Here, we delve into the future trends poised to shape the marketing landscape.

Artificial Intelligence and Personalization

The integration of Artificial Intelligence (AI) and Machine Learning (ML) in marketing strategies is set to deepen. AI's ability to analyze vast datasets enables unprecedented levels of personalization, from content recommendation algorithms akin to Netflix's viewing suggestions to personalized email marketing campaigns that cater to individual consumer preferences. AI-driven chatbots for personalized customer service are becoming standard, enhancing customer experiences while optimizing resource allocation.

Voice Search Optimization

With the increasing use of voice-activated assistants like Amazon's Alexa and Google Assistant, voice search optimization becomes crucial. This trend necessitates a shift in SEO strategies, focusing on natural language processing and long-tail keywords that mirror how people talk rather than type. Brands like Domino's have capitalized on this trend, allowing customers to order pizza through voice commands, showcasing the potential for voice search to simplify consumer interactions.

Augmented Reality (AR) Experiences

Augmented Reality (AR) is transforming the customer experience, offering interactive and immersive ways to engage with products. For instance, IKEA's AR app, Ikea Place, allows customers to visualize furniture in their own space before purchasing. This trend is likely to expand across industries, from fashion to beauty to real estate, as AR technology becomes more accessible and consumers seek richer online shopping experiences.

Sustainability and Ethical Marketing

Consumer demand for sustainability and ethical practices is driving brands to align their marketing strategies with environmental and social values. Patagonia's commitment to sustainability has long been central to its brand identity, resonating with consumers who prioritize environmental conservation. As awareness and concern for global challenges grow, brands that transparently communicate their sustainability efforts and ethical standards will gain consumer trust and loyalty.

Social Commerce and Influencer Collaborations

Social commerce is blurring the lines between social media and e-commerce, as platforms like Instagram and TikTok introduce shopping features directly within their apps. Alongside this, influencer collaborations continue to be a powerful marketing tool, with influencers acting as trusted intermediaries between brands and consumers. The authenticity and reach of influencers, particularly micro-influencers, can significantly impact purchase decisions.

Privacy and Data Protection

In response to increasing concerns about data privacy, marketers must navigate privacy regulations such as GDPR and CCPA while still delivering personalized experiences. This challenge calls for innovative approaches to data collection and usage that respect consumer privacy, such as adopting privacy-first analytics and emphasizing transparency in data practices.

18.2 PIONEERING SUSTAINABLE AND ETHICAL MARKETING APPROACHES

In an era where consumers are increasingly conscientious about the environmental and social impact of their purchases, sustainable and ethical marketing approaches are not just commendable—they're imperative. Businesses are recognizing the necessity to integrate these values into their core strategies to meet consumer expectations, build trust, and foster long-term loyalty. This section explores how pioneering brands are leading the way in sustainable and ethical marketing, setting new standards for the industry.

Emphasizing Transparency and Authenticity

Patagonia's Commitment to Sustainability: Patagonia stands out as a beacon of sustainability and ethical practices in the business world. The company's dedication to environmental conservation is evident in its transparent supply chain, commitment to using recycled materials, and initiatives like the "Worn Wear" program, which encourages consumers to repair, share, and recycle their gear. Patagonia's marketing strategies are deeply intertwined with its mission, demonstrating that profitability and sustainability can go hand in hand.

Leveraging Certifications and Partnerships

Fair Trade and Beyond: Brands like Ben & Jerry's and Tony's Chocolonely use fair trade certifications to underscore their commitment to ethical sourcing and labor practices. These certifications serve as a powerful marketing tool, assuring consumers of the brand's adherence to stringent ethical standards. Furthermore, partnerships with environmental and social organizations can amplify a brand's impact and credibility in sustainability efforts.

Storytelling with Purpose

TOMS Shoes – A Story of Giving: TOMS Shoes has leveraged the power of storytelling to build its brand around a simple yet powerful message: with every purchase, the company will help a person in need. This one-for-one giving model has been central to TOMS' marketing, resonating with consumers who seek to make a positive impact with their purchases. Storytelling that highlights a brand's ethical initiatives can foster emotional connections, turning customers into brand advocates.

Innovating for Sustainability

Beyond Meat – The Future of Protein: Beyond Meat has positioned itself at the forefront of sustainable innovation by offering plant-based meat substitutes that significantly reduce environmental impact compared to traditional meat production. The company's marketing emphasizes the health, environmental, and ethical benefits of plant-based diets, appealing to a broad audience concerned with sustainability, health, and animal welfare.

Engaging Consumers in Sustainability Efforts

Ecosia – Planting Trees with Every Search: Ecosia, a search engine that uses its ad revenue to plant trees, empowers consumers to contribute to reforestation efforts simply by browsing the web. This innovative model demonstrates how companies can engage consumers directly in sustainability initiatives, making environmental action an integral part of the brand experience.

18.3 MARKETING'S FUTURE IN EVOLVING TECHNOLOGIES

The trajectory of marketing is inextricably linked to the evolution of technology. As digital advancements continue to unfold at an unprecedented pace, marketers are provided with new tools and platforms to engage with their audiences more effectively, personalize experiences, and measure the impact of their efforts with greater precision. This section explores how evolving technologies are shaping the future of marketing, highlighting key areas where innovation is driving significant shifts in strategy and execution.

Artificial Intelligence (AI) and Machine Learning (ML)

AI and ML in Personalization and Automation: AI and ML technologies are revolutionizing marketing by enabling hyper-personalized customer experiences and automating decision-making processes. For instance, platforms like Salesforce use AI to help marketers predict customer behaviors, personalize email campaigns, and automate customer service interactions. AI-driven chatbots, like those deployed by Sephora, offer personalized shopping experiences, recommending products based on individual preferences and past behavior.

Augmented Reality (AR) and Virtual Reality (VR)

Enhancing Customer Experiences with AR and VR: AR and VR technologies are transforming the way brands interact with consumers, offering immersive experiences that blur the lines between digital and physical realms. IKEA's AR app, IKEA Place, allows customers to visualize furniture in their homes before making a purchase, enhancing decision-making and reducing returns. Meanwhile, luxury fashion brands like Gucci have embraced AR for virtual try-ons, allowing customers to see how accessories look on them using their smartphone cameras.

Internet of Things (IoT)

IoT for Enhanced Customer Insights and Engagement: The proliferation of IoT devices offers marketers unprecedented access to consumer data and insights, enabling more targeted and context-aware marketing strategies. Smart home devices, wearables, and connected cars collect vast amounts of data, offering clues about consumer preferences, habits, and lifestyles. Brands like Nestlé leverage IoT to offer personalized nutrition advice through smart kitchen devices, creating new touchpoints for customer engagement.

Blockchain Technology

Blockchain for Transparency and Trust: Blockchain technology is beginning to make its mark on marketing, particularly in areas requiring transparency and trust. For instance, IBM's Food Trust network uses blockchain to trace the origin and supply chain of food products, reassuring consumers about the quality and safety of their purchases. In the realm of digital advertising, blockchain can combat fraud, ensure the integrity of ad delivery, and provide transparent transaction records.

5G Connectivity

The Impact of 5G on Marketing Strategies: The rollout of 5G networks is set to revolutionize mobile marketing by significantly enhancing the speed and reliability of mobile connections. This advancement will facilitate richer mobile experiences, support more sophisticated AR and VR applications, and enable real-time data analytics, opening new avenues for mobile engagement and personalized marketing at scale.

18.4 BLOCKCHAIN'S POTENTIAL IN MARKETING

Blockchain technology, best known for underpinning cryptocurrencies like Bitcoin, holds transformative potential beyond the realm of finance. Its features — decentralization, transparency, and security — offer intriguing possibilities for marketing. This section explores how blockchain is poised to influence various aspects of marketing, from enhancing customer trust to revolutionizing loyalty programs and ensuring ad transparency.

Enhancing Consumer Trust and Transparency

Supply Chain Transparency: Blockchain's ability to provide a transparent and immutable ledger of transactions makes it an ideal tool for enhancing supply chain visibility. For instance, IBM's Food Trust uses blockchain to track the journey of food products from farm to table, allowing consumers to verify the origins and handling of their food. This level of transparency builds consumer trust, particularly important for brands emphasizing quality, safety, and sustainability.

Revolutionizing Loyalty Programs

Tokenized Rewards Systems: Traditional loyalty programs often face issues like low engagement and complex redemption processes. Blockchain offers a solution through tokenized rewards that can be easily tracked, transferred, and redeemed across a network of partners without the need for intermediaries. Singapore Airlines' KrisPay is a pioneering example, allowing frequent flyers to convert their miles into digital currency that can be spent with various retail partners, simplifying and enhancing the value of loyalty rewards.

Combating Ad Fraud

Ad Transparency and Verification: The digital advertising ecosystem is fraught with inefficiencies and fraud, including bot traffic and misrepresented ad delivery metrics. Blockchain can address these challenges by providing a transparent ledger for ad transactions, enabling advertisers to verify that their ads are displayed as intended and that engagement metrics are genuine. Aqilliz, a blockchain solutions provider, partners with brands to facilitate transparent ad verification, ensuring that marketing budgets are spent effectively.

Facilitating Secure and Private Customer Data Management

Decentralized Data Management: In an era where data privacy concerns are paramount, blockchain offers a decentralized approach to data storage and management. This ensures enhanced security and gives consumers control over their data. Civic is an example of how blockchain can be used for identity verification, allowing users to control and securely share their personal information with businesses, streamlining processes like customer onboarding while respecting privacy.

Enabling Direct and Transparent Consumer Transactions

Smart Contracts for Direct Sales: Blockchain enables the use of smart contracts — self-executing contracts with the terms of the agreement directly written into code. This can facilitate direct transactions between businesses and consumers without intermediaries, potentially lowering costs and increasing efficiency. For example, artists and creators use blockchain platforms like Ethereum to sell their work directly to fans, ensuring authenticity and fair compensation.

CHAPTER 19. CONCLUDING INSIGHTS: REFLECTIONS AND FUTURE PERSPECTIVES

As we reach the culmination of our journey through the multifaceted realm of marketing, "Concluding Insights: Reflections and Future Perspectives" serves as a reflective mirror and a forward-looking lens. This chapter synthesizes the wealth of knowledge and insights garnered throughout the exploration of marketing's evolution, its current state, and the potential trajectories it may follow in the face of unrelenting technological advancements, shifting consumer expectations, and the ever-growing imperatives of sustainability and ethical considerations.

The chapter begins by revisiting the transformative shifts in marketing practices from traditional methodologies to the complex, digitally-driven ecosystem we navigate today. It underscores the critical learnings distilled from these transitions, emphasizing the integration of consistent messaging across myriad platforms, the inevitable pivot towards digital engagement, and the paramount importance of data-driven decision-making in crafting personalized, impactful marketing strategies.

Reflecting on the lessons learned, the narrative shifts to underscore the significance of sustainability and ethical marketing in today's business environment.

In an era marked by increased consumer consciousness about environmental and social issues, brands like Patagonia exemplify how integrating sustainability and ethical practices into marketing strategies not only aligns with consumer expectations but also fosters deeper, more meaningful connections with the audience.

The discourse then navigates through the implications of emerging technologies such as AI, AR/VR, and blockchain on the marketing landscape. These innovations promise to redefine engagement strategies, offering new ways to personalize experiences, enhance consumer interactions, and ensure transparency and trust in brand-consumer relationships.

Looking ahead, the chapter speculates on the future of marketing practice, envisioning a domain where hyper-personalization, driven by advanced technological capabilities, becomes the norm. It anticipates a marketing ecosystem where ethical marketing and sustainability are not just differentiators but foundational pillars of brand identity, urging marketers to embrace continuous learning and adaptability as indispensable competencies for navigating the complexities of the modern marketplace. This concluding chapter not only encapsulates the core insights from the evolution of marketing but also inspires a contemplative outlook towards embracing the challenges and opportunities that lie ahead. It encourages marketers to forge paths that are not only innovative and impactful but also ethically grounded and sustainability-oriented, thereby contributing to a more equitable and sustainable future.

19.1 SYNTHESIZING KEY TAKEAWAYS FROM MARKETING EVOLUTION

The evolution of marketing from its traditional roots to the complex digital ecosystem of today offers profound insights into how businesses can connect with consumers, adapt to changes, and achieve sustainable growth. This journey has been marked by significant shifts in technology, consumer behavior, and societal values, each shaping the strategies and tools marketers use. Reflecting on this evolution, several key takeaways emerge, encapsulating lessons learned and guiding principles for the future.

Integration and Consistency are Crucial

The rise of integrated marketing communications (IMC) underscores the importance of delivering a consistent and unified brand message across all channels and touchpoints. The Dove "Real Beauty" campaign exemplifies this approach, demonstrating how consistent messaging across platforms can resonate deeply with audiences, drive engagement, and foster brand loyalty.

The Digital Shift is Inevitable

The transition to digital marketing is not just a trend but a fundamental shift in how businesses engage with consumers. The digital landscape offers unparalleled opportunities for targeting, personalization, and measurement. Brands like Nike, with its innovative digital campaigns and direct-to-consumer focus, illustrate the effectiveness of embracing digital channels to enhance brand visibility and consumer connection.

Data-Driven Insights Drive Success

The advent of big data and analytics has transformed marketing into a data-driven discipline. The ability to collect, analyze, and act on data allows marketers to understand consumer behaviors, preferences, and trends more deeply than ever before. This shift towards data-driven strategies enables more personalized and effective marketing efforts, as seen in Spotify's use of listening data to create personalized playlists.

Sustainability and Ethics Matter More Than Ever

Consumer awareness and concern for environmental and social issues have placed sustainability and ethics at the forefront of marketing. Brands that prioritize and authentically communicate their commitment to these values, like Patagonia, not only align with consumer expectations but also build stronger, more meaningful relationships with their audience.

Technology Continues to Reshape Marketing

Emerging technologies such as AI, AR/VR, and blockchain are set to further revolutionize marketing, offering new ways to engage consumers, enhance experiences, and ensure transparency. The use of AR in IKEA's Place app for visualizing furniture in customers' homes is a prime example of how technology can solve real consumer problems and enhance the decision-making process.

Case Study: Spotify's Use of Data Analytics for Personalization

Background: Spotify, a leader in the music streaming industry, leverages big data and machine learning to offer personalized music recommendations to its users, creating a highly individualized listening experience.

Application: By analyzing vast amounts of data on user preferences, listening habits, and even the time of day, Spotify curates personalized playlists for each user, such as the Discover Weekly playlist. This approach has significantly increased user engagement and retention.

Future Implication: Spotify's success with data-driven personalization exemplifies the importance of leveraging technology to understand and cater to individual customer needs, a trend that will continue to dominate the marketing landscape.

19.2 ENVISIONING THE FUTURE OF MARKETING PRACTICE

As we reflect on the transformative journey of marketing, it becomes evident that the discipline is on the cusp of another significant evolution. The convergence of technological advancements, changing consumer dynamics, and a heightened emphasis on sustainability and ethical practices are crafting a new frontier for marketing. Envisioning the future of marketing practice involves understanding these shifts and preparing to navigate the opportunities and challenges they present.

Hyper-Personalization Through Advanced Technologies

The future of marketing lies in hyper-personalization, powered by advancements in AI and machine learning. As technology becomes more sophisticated, brands will have the ability to not only anticipate customer needs but also tailor experiences in real-time, offering unparalleled relevance and value to each individual. The integration of AI with emerging technologies like AR and VR will create immersive and personalized marketing experiences that bridge the digital and physical worlds.

Ethical Marketing and Sustainability as Core Pillars

Consumer demand for transparency, sustainability, and ethical conduct is shaping marketing strategies. In the future, these elements will become not just differentiators but essential components of brand identity. Marketers will increasingly use their platforms to address global challenges, contributing to a positive social and environmental impact. Brands that can authentically integrate these values into their marketing practices, similar to Patagonia's approach, will foster deeper connections with their audiences.

Seamless Omnichannel Experiences

The distinction between online and offline channels will continue to blur, giving rise to truly seamless omnichannel experiences. The future of marketing practice will involve creating cohesive customer journeys that fluidly transition between digital and physical touchpoints. Technologies like IoT and 5G will play crucial roles in enabling these integrated experiences, offering marketers new ways to engage with consumers across multiple channels simultaneously.

Leveraging Data While Prioritizing Privacy

As data remains a cornerstone of effective marketing, balancing its use with privacy concerns will be paramount. The future will likely see the development of new frameworks and technologies that allow marketers to leverage consumer data for personalization while strictly adhering to privacy regulations and ethical standards. Blockchain technology could offer solutions for secure, transparent data management, ensuring consumer trust in how their information is used.

Continuous Learning and Adaptability

The rapid pace of change in technology and consumer preferences will require marketers to embrace continuous learning and adaptability as core competencies. Staying ahead will mean not only keeping abreast of the latest digital tools and platforms but also cultivating an agile mindset that can quickly respond to market shifts. Future marketing professionals will need to balance creative thinking with analytical prowess, leveraging data to inform strategies while pushing the boundaries of innovation.

Case Study: IKEA's Integration of AR Technology

Background: IKEA introduced an AR app, IKEA Place, allowing customers to visualize furniture in their own space before making a purchase, addressing a common customer pain point in the furniture buying process.

Application: By using AR technology, IKEA not only enhanced the customer experience but also reduced the friction in the buying process, leading to increased satisfaction and decreased return rates.

Future Implication: IKEA's use of AR for solving practical customer problems illustrates how emerging technologies can be harnessed to improve the customer journey, a strategy that will become increasingly important as new technologies develop.

19.3 FUTURE SKILLS AND COMPETENCIES IN MARKETING

As the marketing landscape continues to evolve under the influence of rapid technological advancements, shifting consumer expectations, and an increasing focus on sustainability and ethics, the skill set required for marketing professionals is also transforming. The future of marketing will demand a blend of technical knowledge, strategic thinking, creativity, and ethical judgment. Understanding and developing these competencies will be crucial for marketers aiming to navigate the complexities of the modern marketplace successfully. Here, we explore the key skills and competencies that will define the future of marketing practice.

Technological Proficiency

Overview: The integration of emerging technologies like AI, AR/VR, and IoT into marketing strategies necessitates a deep understanding of these tools and their applications.

Competencies:

Data Analytics and Insights: Ability to analyze data to derive actionable insights for personalized marketing strategies.

Digital Platforms Mastery: Proficiency in utilizing digital and social media platforms for optimized content delivery and engagement.

Strategic and Analytical Thinking

Overview: The dynamic marketing environment requires the ability to think strategically, analyze market trends, and adapt strategies accordingly.

Competencies:

Agile Strategy Development: Capacity to develop flexible strategies that can quickly adapt to changes in the market or consumer behavior.

Critical Analysis: Skill in evaluating the effectiveness of marketing campaigns and identifying areas for improvement.

Creative and Innovative Problem-Solving

Overview: Creativity remains at the heart of marketing, crucial for developing compelling campaigns and innovative solutions to engage consumers.

Competencies:

Content Creation: Crafting engaging, original content that resonates with target audiences.

Innovative Thinking: Ability to leverage new technologies and trends to create unique marketing opportunities and solutions.

Ethical Judgment and Sustainability Awareness

Overview: As consumers increasingly value ethical practices and sustainability, marketers must incorporate these considerations into their strategies.

Competencies:

Ethical Marketing Practices: Understanding and applying ethical considerations in marketing strategies, ensuring transparency and fairness.

Sustainability Integration: Ability to develop marketing campaigns that promote and support sustainable practices, aligning with consumer values and contributing to a positive social impact.

Emotional Intelligence and Customer-Centricity

Overview: Understanding and empathizing with consumer needs and emotions are crucial for building strong relationships and delivering personalized experiences.

Competencies:

Empathy: Ability to understand and respond to the emotional needs and concerns of consumers.

Customer Engagement: Skills in creating meaningful interactions and building loyalty through personalized communication and experiences.

Continuous Learning and Adaptability

Overview: The rapid pace of change in marketing necessitates a commitment to continuous learning and the flexibility to adapt to new challenges and opportunities.

Competencies:

Learning Agility: Willingness and ability to learn new skills and adapt to new technologies and market trends.

Resilience and Flexibility: Capacity to navigate setbacks and changes in the marketing landscape with a positive attitude and an openness to new approaches.

Case Study: Patagonia's Commitment to Sustainability

Background: Patagonia, an outdoor apparel company, has long been committed to environmental sustainability, making it a core aspect of its brand identity and marketing strategy.

Application: Patagonia's marketing campaigns often focus on environmental activism, such as the "Don't Buy This Jacket" campaign that encouraged consumers to consider the environmental impact of their purchases. The company also invests in sustainable practices, such as using recycled materials and encouraging product repairs.

Future Implication: Patagonia's blending of marketing with sustainability and ethical practices showcases the growing importance of aligning brand values with consumer concerns about the environment and society. Marketers of the future will need to navigate these values authentically and creatively.

What is Special About this Book!

"Marketing: Theory, Practice, and Perspectives" stands out as a comprehensive and forward-thinking resource in the field of marketing for several reasons:

Depth and Breadth of Content: This book covers an extensive range of topics from foundational theories to the latest in digital marketing strategies. This breadth ensures that readers gain a holistic understanding of marketing as both a practice and an evolving discipline.

Integration of Theory and Practice: Balancing theoretical insights with practical applications, the book becomes a valuable resource for both students learning about marketing and professionals applying these concepts in real-world scenarios.

Emphasis on Ethical and Sustainable Marketing: Addressing ethics and social responsibility, particularly in the context of global challenges, aligns the book with current industry trends and societal expectations, making it highly relevant in today's market.

Advanced Marketing Practices and Digital Integration: The focus on digital marketing, AI, VR, and mobile marketing reflects the cutting-edge of the industry. Given the rapid technological advancements and their impact on marketing, this focus is especially pertinent.

Data-Driven Marketing Insights: Emphasizing the leveraging of marketing analytics, understanding ROI, and ethics in data-driven marketing aligns with the growing trend of basing marketing decisions on data analysis and measurable outcomes.

Global Perspective and Cultural Sensitivity: The book's coverage of global marketing strategies and cross-cultural marketing acknowledges the importance of globalization in marketing, making it an essential read for marketers in an increasingly interconnected world.

Adaptation to Current Trends: The book's content, such as addressing digital transformation, evolving consumer preferences, and the challenges of marketing in a tech-driven world, mirrors the current industry landscape, making it a timely and relevant resource.

Future-Oriented Approach: Exploring future trends and potential directions, such as the impact of blockchain technology, the book not only educates about current practices but also prepares readers for emerging developments.

Case Studies and Real-World Examples: The inclusion of case studies enhances understanding by providing real-world context. This approach aids in bridging the gap between theory and practice.

In comparison with other marketing books and resources, "Marketing: Theory, Practice, and Perspectives" offers a unique blend of comprehensive coverage, practical application, ethical consideration, and forward-looking insights. This positions it as a valuable resource for both students new to marketing and seasoned professionals seeking to update their knowledge with the latest trends and technologies in the field.

9798883764966

www.ingramcontent.com/pod-product-compliance
Lightning Source LLC
Chambersburg PA
CBHW071034290526
45795CB00004B/1200